*naked
into
the
night*

For Sue,

~~Dear~~ friend from
the Granby class of 1959.
Thanks for your
support of my
literature.
This set is for you.
Love,

Monty

30 April 2009

naked into the night

a novel

monty joynes

HAMPTON ROADS
PUBLISHING COMPANY, INC.

Cover design by Marjoram Productions

For information write:

Hampton Roads Publishing Company, Inc.
134 Burgess Lane
Charlottesville, VA 22902

Or call: (804) 296-2772
FAX: (804) 296-5096
e-mail: hrpc@mail.hamptonroadspub.com
Web site: http://www.hamptonroadspub.com

If you are unable to order this book from your local
bookseller, you may order directly from the publisher.
Quantity discounts for organizations are available.
Call 1-800-766-8009, toll-free.

ISBN 1-57174-055-4

10 9 8 7 6 5 4 3 2 1

Printed in Canada

To the elder brothers:
Jesus of Nazareth,
Ramana Maharshi,
and J. Krishnamurti.

CHAPTER ONE

Mid-May in Norfolk, Virginia, can be rainy and chilly, especially in the early morning. The Chesapeake Bay is still cold from winter, and Norfolk's Ocean View beaches do not see comfortable swimmers until mid-June. In Lakewood, the upscale neighborhood where Winston lived, the fog from a branch of the Lafayette River had obscured the Conovers' boat dock and rolled up the long sloping backyard. The drizzling rain and fog kept most people indoors until time to leave for work. The smart folks had rolled their large trash containers to the curb the night before so that they wouldn't have to get up at seven in an attempt to beat the garbage truck. Wednesday the 17th was a garbage pick-up day in Lakewood.

Subconsciously, Winston knew it was garbage pick-up day, but household details were far from his mind. In fact, in recent days, Winston had made a concerted effort to empty his mind. In the weeks prior to the 17th there had been a cacophony of voices dialoguing in his awareness. The conversations between various aspects of himself—and he did recognize them as parts of self—often turned

argumentative, even violent. Much of the unwanted
chatter dealt with harsh criticisms of himself and
the society his generation had created. The diatribes
were more against institutions than individuals.
Strangely, Ellen and the children were exempt. They
were protected behind walls of rationalization.

Winston had already solved the dilemma of family. He was not abandoning them, at least not in
the way delinquent fathers abandon wives and children to face destitution. This father was leaving behind everything that seemed important to Ellen,
Buffy, and Theo. The kids had gotten their formal
education. Well, at least as much as they would tolerate. Buffy was married, working, with no plans for
a child of her own. Theo, who had gone to Maine
to clip birch branches rather than come into the
family business, was finally being successful at
something: real estate sales in the Vermont resort
condominium market. Even Theo must have seen the
irony of that, since he could have been doing the
same thing in Virginia Beach, selling properties
under the management of Conover Real Estate, Inc.
Or he could have made a living just supervising the
three automated car washes owned by his parents.

The Conover corporation had had quite a few
good years. There was a great deal of equity in the
Lakewood house, their office buildings, and a condo
at Nags Head on the North Carolina Outer Banks.
The car washes, the Cadillac, and the Ford Explorer
were paid off, and there was a retirement portfolio
of mutuals, IRAs, and stocks that, if left alone,
would provide a rich lifestyle for Ellen even if she

lived to be 100. As far as Winston was concerned, he had met all of his family obligations.

With regard to further paternal nurturing, Buffy and Theo had been forthright in telling him that they had their own lives and that they no longer desired his judgments or advice. Contact and conversations were now restricted to platitudes lest an emotional blowup ruin an event. Sometimes his children seemed like strangers, and Winston wondered whether if he met them socially he would even like or respect them. He regretted that the answer was probably not.

When the idea of leaving naked into the night came to Winston, his mind played out a variety of fantasies about how the escape might be practically accomplished. How would he avoid the humiliation of having it end on the rear seat of a police car, his hands cuffed rudely behind his back, off balance and prone on cold vinyl seat covers with only a coarse emergency blanket thrown over to make him less offensive to strangers?

"Don't you dare pee in my patrol car. Do you hear me?" In his imagination, he could see the cop's heavy black belt and creased pants and hear the castigation through the rear door just before it slammed shut.

And if he got away, where would he go? He was too old for the French Foreign Legion. And besides not being able to pass the physical, he had no respect for the French or their wars. Service to Mother Teresa was an option, but how would he get to India? And what if he got there and she turned out to be a tyrant? He couldn't join a monastery. He was neither Catholic nor desirous of becoming one. There seemed to be no cause that was completely virtuous. Religious leaders and charities built empires of self-aggrandizement, power, and wealth. Even the United Community Fund and the Red Cross with its tainted blood put the prosperity and security of their leadership before the function of their organizations. What institution was worthy of his devotion? Where could he go to sacrifice himself? Were there any objectives left to middle-aged American martyrs? What action was possible to make a single life worth living? The process of this thinking led to the choices of suicide or murder.

Suicide was a protest. But if you were going to protest that strongly, rather than kill yourself, why not kill the object of protest? That's how some disoriented, dispossessed individuals decide to kill a president or a pope. They project all of their disillusion and frustration on a public figure. The attempt at murder is also an attempt at suicide. People who are willing to die are also willing to kill. But Winston was not willing to die. He wanted to surrender more than he wanted to attack.

Living well was supposed to be the best revenge. Yes, he could abscond with the assets of his family and live very comfortably in a warm country that would not extradite him back to the United States. He could hang out at the beach bars and satiate himself with sex from beautiful but poor young women in string bikinis. He could indulge himself for a time in forgetfulness. But hadn't that been what he had done his entire life? Isn't a fantasy just another kind of idea? Another plan? And what if it were achieved like so many of his plans? The achievement was not an end. It never brought peace. It never sustained happiness. If he had learned one thing, it was that there was no real happiness in achieving your dreams. Dreams were just replaced with other dreams and the cycle of seeking and obtaining went on and on.

Too often Winn's thoughts became directed anger. He couldn't blame himself for every disappointment, so he projected his rage on two inventions that had dominated his generation: automobiles and television. One day, he came to the conclusion that he could never drive a vehicle again. Driving had long ago ceased to be an adventure or even a reliable pleasure. Driving every day in Norfolk and Virginia Beach had become a misery, a guaranteed dose of stress. Avoiding accidents could only be computed as luck. Young women seemed to be dangerously assertive on the interstates. Senior citizens seemed shriveled behind their wheels, watching the speed limit as if it were taking them too fast to a cemetery. Groups of teenagers were always going to a happening, and the reward for observing them too long was a display of middle fingers and recognizable profanities that could be read on their lips. No one, it appeared, observed the posted speed limit. No one was considerate behind the wheel of his car. No one cared about the pollution. Driving a car seemed indispensable to life itself, no matter whom or what it killed incidentally. If Winn was going to remake himself as a human being, he felt that he must first renounce the automobile.

The second great renunciation was television. In Winn's final view, television had killed culture. If Winn had a literary hero, it was Carl Sandburg. He had once written a paper on Sandburg in the only college literature course he had taken. On a vacation to the Smokey Mountains, he had even detoured to the Sandburg home in East Flat Rock, North Carolina. He discovered that the aging man, one of the originators of innately American literature, sat often in an attic room amid stacks of *Life* magazines and favorite record albums. Sandburg's window on the world was not television, with its instant views of war and politics, its predigested history, and its sex and violence ideas of entertainment.

Television would never nourish profound minds or creative ideas. Television, even with its best documentaries, would not promote intellect. It filled the mind with chatter, superficial distractions from the true voices of life. Television separated real people from each other. It made them strangers in their own living rooms. One watched sports in one room while the mate watched a romantic movie in another. If television programming homogenized society with a common experience, it made the common experience mediocre, or worse . . . it made its viewers mean and impatient for immediate gratification of their base desires. Its examples killed social manners and overfed the libido with incessant stimulation. Television pandered like a seducer. It lured the public away from consideration and kindness, into a world of sexual fantasy. Fortunes were made by producers and performers who pandered to the hormonal stimulation of pubescent adolescents. Women undressed to seduce, and men, demonstrating their sexual hunger, acted out the copulation ritual as popular entertainment. The same people then refused to be responsible for the rise in illegitimate childbirths and rape and the increase of venereal disease and AIDS.

A country becomes what it admires. When television news programming began to devote itself to the lives of entertainment personalities, Winn recognized that the insanity was contagious. The vector was not sexual contact. It was not airborne or carried by insects or rats. The great sickness was carried on unseen electronic impulses that broadcast into every home. The spread of it was absolutely insidious.

Perhaps an alien species had infected Earth with the television disease as a means of destroying its will and abilities. Rather than destroy physically, they slowly dissolved culture. With no viable society, Earth could be conquered at leisure. Perhaps humans were being cultivated as a food source for the equivalent of alien pet dogs and cats. Such an alien destiny for Earth would be at least certain and useful. The destiny that Earth had inarticulated for itself was much less certain or even functional. Earth worshiped personal pleasure and power. Its collective destiny was only one generation away. From its orientation, destiny ended with death or bankruptcy. Could Sandburg find a Lincoln in such an environment? If television were a reflection of reality, Winn wanted no further exposure to it.

Most urbanized Americans cursed traffic and television during their lives and threatened to quit them. But name the ones who did. Winston Conover took that radical step. He took it and kept on walking, without so much as a pair of socks or a credit card.

People who knew the old Winston would have named him last on a list of those most likely to walk out of their lives buck naked. Winn was considered a regular guy, a stable, successful guy. Look at where he came from, and you'd never figure Winn for a stunt like that.

Winn was more a social personality than a leader in high school or college. He maintained a B average and had a natural ability in math, but seldom pressed the accelerator of his intellect. Although he was elected president of his Granby High senior class, the recognition was largely due to his ability to acquire every new dance step of the late fifties, which he enthusiastically demonstrated at school dances and parties. He needed his father's influence to get into the University of Virginia. His father owned an insurance agency with a few clients who were important UVA alumni.

Winn majored in business and Sigma Nu, the jock fraternity, at Virginia. Although he was six feet tall and could always carry weight on a muscular frame, he saw athletics as a poor investment of energy unless you were a star and sought a professional career. Winn learned this lesson in high school after a season of junior varsity football. He was not star material.

Among the relative football and basketball giants at Sigma Nu, Winn was pledged for academic and social balance. As soon as he declared as a business major, the fraternity voted him House Manager. In the years that Winn managed Sigma Nu, his accounting books, party band contracts, and arbitration skills stood out as one area of solid ground amid a riotous, earthquake-prone house. It was Winn who defended the house before the dean of the University on charges of regular showings of "fuck flicks" to which admission was charged. In his senior year, a grateful fraternity named Winn its president.

Like many men in his 1963 graduating class, Winn sought the protection of graduate school to avoid being drafted into the army. He was able to stretch an MBA out to four semesters. His family was financially supportive, Sigma Nu kept rocking, and he had two or three serious romances. Winn remembered the mid-sixties as the most carefree days of his life. The day after he walked the Lawn between Jefferson's Rotunda and Cabell Hall for a second degree, he was sworn in to the Virginia National Guard. His father had arranged it through a good client who happened to also be the commanding officer of a National Guard unit. For the next six years, Winn served as the company clerk in an artillery unit. He achieved the rank of Specialist Fourth Class.

Winn spent the summer of 1965 enjoying the girls and the beach at Virginia Beach. The National

Guard colonel put Winn's Basic Training date off to give him time to get in better shape. His college beer diet had ballooned him to 190 pounds. He hit Fort Gordon, Georgia, at 180 and graduated Basic at 164. The horrors of wartime army Basic Training formed the basis of some of Winn's best stories. Through them he allayed the guilt of not going to the Vietnam war, and established a rapport with those who did.

The association with his father's insurance agency lasted less than two years. Winn did not enjoy the selling of an abstract service. He did not like the cold calling and the fishing for clients at every social encounter. Most of all, he did not like the math on building a commission base; he calculated that he could not reach a six-figure income until his father retired. Then, too, Norfolk had its social problems and there was white flight to more distant suburbs. Virginia Beach was one of the fastest growing cities in the entire country, and Chesapeake with its huge land area was ripe for industrial development. The place to be in 1968 in the Tidewater, Virginia, area was real estate. Winn did his homework and had a real estate license two weeks before his father agreed to let him go.

Winn joined a new firm formed by three hot-shot salesmen who also saw the gold-plated future in commercial real estate. Sure, there was good money in residential sales, but the big scores were in commercial properties. Sell a big house and you could make thousands. Sell an office building or a motel property and you could make tens of thousands. Develop a shopping center and assume its lease management and you could make hundreds of thousands.

As the junior associate, Winn began on the periphery of the major deals, but within a year, using the old boy network of native familiarity, fraternity contacts, and his father's referrals, he was closing contracts on impressive commercial listings.

The next year Winn got into six figures by living his business. He hardly knew the day of the week without resorting to his appointment calendar. The only complaint about Winn from his associates and clients was that he called them either too early in the morning or too late at night. Winn had a telephone in his car in 1969, when such an installation was an expensive novelty.

Ellen came into Winn's life that same year. She was a residential sales associate of another firm. Her listing was a farmhouse and property that Winn needed to complete a housing development parcel in Princess Anne. The parcel was key to the deal, but the seller had to be kept in the dark. Winn needed to option the property without disclosing the intentions of the developers.

Winn knew Ellen only as a professional voice on the phone when they agreed to meet for breakfast to discuss the sale of the farm property. He was so pleased by her appearance that he thought as much about dating her as selling her. Ellen was two years out of Madison College, a Harrisonburg, Virginia, women's college where UVA men dated when they could not shake the status trees at Sweetbriar or Hollins. Ellen had been informally engaged to a cadet at Virginia Military Institute. The passion of college weekends cooled when they graduated and the army conspired to keep them apart. Ellen returned to her home in Virginia Beach and found that she had an interest and aptitude in selling houses. Her career was a compensation for the infrequent weekends with her infantry lieutenant. She told him that she could find a job selling real estate anywhere they were stationed. But when he got orders to a California base and reasoned that he could not send for her or support her, the engagement ended. Ellen had no ring to return. The disappointment was something she had suspected, but the hurt was still real. This was followed by a long month of anger and recrimination. Then she met Winn.

Winn struck her romantic imagination from the moment he introduced himself. He was not what she expected. Most of the men that Ellen had met in real estate were not attractive. They may have dressed in sport coats and ties, but showing properties all day made them appear always worn. To her, real estate salesmen meant scuffed shoes, baggy pants, crummy complexions, bad ties, and cigarette breath. In contrast, Winn looked like a walking ad for good suits. He was really "put together," as Ellen would tell her mother. The navy blue suit was a classic, tailored at Shulman's in downtown Norfolk to complement a man who carried 184 pounds without a bulge of excess. The shirt and tie were of equal quality, and the Johnston & Murphy shoes were purchased at the same fitting to complete the successful executive look. Knowing that he must appear the equal of whomever he did business with, Winn considered his wardrobe and his weekly hair styling (at three times the rate working-class men paid for haircuts) a career investment.

"If you want to do business with millionaire developers," Winn told his associates, "you have to look like you belong among them. If you don't look sharp, they will automatically question your ability."

There was another advantage to Winn's appearance that had always served him well in an ego-centered culture, especially among men. Winn did not possess the facial features of a movie star. His forehead was a little too high, his ears a bit too large, his hair a shade too mousy brown and on the thin side. When concentrating, Winn had two habits that unbalanced whatever symmetry his face might have had. He either rolled his lower lip to his chin in an exaggerated pout, or he jutted his mouth to the right to such an extreme that it made his right eye appear to twitch. Having a serious face-to-face conversation with Winn was like watching him perform facial gymnastics. Men who knew him teased him about the unconscious habits. Women who loved him found them to be endearing. The net effect of Winn's acceptable looks and facial idiosyncrasies was that he was not perceived as competitively threatening to men. In the presence of a beautiful woman, other men always assumed that they would be chosen for their good looks over Winn. They were comfortable around him. They were never reluctant to introduce Winn to their wives, lovers, or prospective girlfriends.

Winn charmed Ellen into a sweetheart real estate sale and then into his bed. Their associates agreed that they were made for each other. A sage giving advice about marriage warned that one should know where one is going before one decides who will be going along. There was no doubt where both Winn and Ellen wanted to go. They wanted to go into the world of real estate. A year after they were married, they established their own firm. Winn worked commercial; Ellen did residential. Ten years later, Conover Real Estate had four offices and nearly fifty employees. The firm might have become larger and richer, but neither Winn nor Ellen was a risk taker. They always preferred to work with client money rather than with their own. Then too, both ultimately reached their levels of administrative ability. While they were excellent at managing their own time, they did not do well at managing the time and productivity of their associates. Both were outside salespeople who hated the confines of the office. Both disliked paperwork and record keeping. Two of their bookkeepers embezzled from them. One loss in an escrow account caused them to lose one of their suburban offices. When a second fraud was discovered some twelve years later, Conover Real Estate consolidated into two locations and cut its sales and office staff to a number Winn and Ellen felt they could control.

Ellen acquired a hard edge in dealing with employees as a result of the losses. Winn chose instead to avoid the office even more than he had in the past and to have both his office manager and his accountant bonded as insurance against future loss. As long as Winn had deals in the works, he was motivated. Whenever Ellen complained about carrying the administrative load of their businesses, Winn reminded her that he was the firm's chief income producer and that he needed to be free to be on the street.

"I'm a salesman," he would remind her. "You don't make sales behind a desk."

"Well, what about my sales?" she would retort. "If I'm showing property, who is going to mind the store?"

"Hire somebody. Delegate the administrative stuff."

"Sure," Ellen would say, knowing that Winn had no idea of what she did every day just to keep the offices staffed and running. Secretly, she did not feel confident in her role as a boss, and she resented Winn's abdication of that role. He should be the one hiring and firing. He should be the one dealing with absences, resignations, and poor performances. He should be working with the CPA. He should be doing the quarterly tax reports. He had no idea about her responsibilities. Winn made wide passes with the brush, in Ellen's picture of their business relationship. She did all the filling in. She was consigned to the drudgery of the details.

Ellen was a pretty girl at twenty-one. She stayed attractive into her thirties although she had a constant battle with her weight. At five feet three, a vacation cruise or any Christmas would automatically attach fat to her buttocks and thighs. When she was busy showing houses all day, often skipping lunch, she kept trim. As her office time increased, so did her weight. She invested in every diet. Even took shots. But year by year, she began to resemble her mother, a matronly size twenty. Ellen had felt disgraced when she had to go to a size twelve. At size fourteen, she experienced a crisis of self-worth. Three years into size sixteen, she decided to punish Winn by buying the most expensive dresses she could find.

Ellen was still a size sixteen when Winn disappeared. Not that he knew her dress size or saw her any differently than when he had married her. He was too busy resenting his own body and the twenty or more suits that he refused to give away but could no longer wear.

Winn had lost the battle of the bulges sooner than Ellen, although his wardrobe had concealed his weight better. At 200 pounds, coats still fit, but pants had to be altered. At 215, the gut was evident but not pronounced. At 230, Winn was referring to himself as a fat man. At 240, he refused to be seen in a pair of shorts.

On the night of May 17, with his weight at 239, Winn's stomach lead the way naked into the night. The face was heavy but not jowly. The forehead was higher, the hair still thin, but there was no sign of balding. There were brown age spots on his hands and the tan of days in the sun ran up to the short sleeve shirt line. His face and neck were also tanned. Open shirts had left a kind of yoke down the front of his chest. He was moderately hairy and very, very white. His back and behind and legs would have seemed bleached white in the glare of some headlight.

A doctor, or even a carnival guesser of ages, would have judged Winn to be middle-aged.

"Yea, middle-aged if the guy lived to be a 104. He's fifty-two or three if he's a day."

Actually, Winn Conover was fifty-four years of age when he awkwardly walked into the fog. The grass was wet and cold beneath his feet, but not uncomfortable. Then he stepped on small rocks in the street and uttered the first words of his new life.

"Ow, ooh. Ooh, ow."

CHAPTER TWO

It is a fact that Winston Conover did on the night of May 17, 1995, remove the tee shirt and boxer shorts in which he had slept and at approximately 1:45 A.M. did exit the front door of his suburban home completely naked. He had not provided for his journey in any way that the authorities could ascertain. He had left no notes. No articles of personal clothing or jewelry were missing. His wallet and identification were on the bureau top where he usually left them overnight. There were no suspicious withdrawals of funds from his bank accounts. The local underworld had not issued a phony driver's license or Social Security card to anyone resembling Conover. If he had any hidden resources or romantic liaisons, they could not be found. And since there were no comets reported the night of the 17th, and no neighbors had observed any intense white lights around the Conover residence, even alien abduction seemed superfluous.

Winston's wife Ellen and his two children, Buffy and Theo, were initially convinced that Winston was kidnapped. A television show concerned with missing persons briefly looked into the case, but could find no drama to propel a feature story. The police thought that Winston just walked away like a growing number of men of his generation. He was not crazy in the legal sense. Sure, to a cop on a salary, working a second job, a guy making $200,000 a year, with most of his assets in equity, and retirement on the horizon, a guy like that would have to be nuts to walk away. But it happens, and with no physical evidence of violence, how long can a case stay open?

A psychologist whom Ellen Conover consulted during her few months of grief came as close to the truth as anyone, but in discussing the notion, Ellen characterized it as "philosophical bullshit." The psychologist suggested that Winston may have been a casualty of Progress, the externalized-culture of the West. In spite of external success, the inward person remains the same—immature, undeveloped. When the hunt for external goods does not prove to be the source of happiness, the inner person begins to raise its claim. One's insatiability amid so much abundance leads to serious disturbances of balance in the mind. One side of the mind perceives the greedy restlessness of its other side. The purpose of life itself comes into question. Guilt and self-doubt ravage the thought system.

"Of course," Ellen had reminded the psychologist. "It's called mid-life crisis and menopause. But there are pills for those conditions, right? I know what that is all about. I had a hysterectomy two years ago."

Life must go on. Every television viewer in the United States knew the foibles of the human personality. Every prejudice and perversion had been exposed, talked about, and offered as entertainment. So what if anybody's brother was killed on the street. Somebody should have been more careful. In this life, you cut your losses and moved on. Movement was the key. The nastiness of trouble couldn't hit you if you were moving. Moving up the social ladder. Moving up the ladder of fame. Moving to a better house or moving up to a more expensive car. The United States was a society of movers. Everybody was moving on. And if you were not there on moving day, you got left behind, and ultimately forgotten. Ask anyone. That's the way it was. That's the way it was supposed to be.

That's what Ellen Conover figured out. Winston was gone. For whatever reason. There would be hell to pay straightening out the finances without a death certificate, but the attorneys could figure that out. Ellen had a business to run. She had been Winston's equal partner, and she knew that she could make a good living. She would have to hire people to do what Winston had done in commercial sales, but even that might work out in the long run. She did not feel threatened. She felt embarrassed. Then she felt angry. He had better be dead, because if he had just walked out of the marriage and business on a whim or a woman, she would kill him if he returned. Well, she would certainly divorce him.

But Winston Conover might not be coming home. He was on an adventure. He was not escaping from something. He was rather coming into the light of himself. Reinventing himself. Like a new baby, he was exploring the world. Trying to find meaning among the vague clues that sensations offer.

In the history of enlightened men who have become world teachers, there are rare cases in which a single step has led to transformation. In India in 1897, a seventeen-year-old middle class boy named Venkataraman Ayyar, unaccustomed to sickness and untrained in spiritual philosophy, lay down on the floor of his uncle's house in a sudden violent fear of death.

The shock of the fear of death drove his mind inward. Without actually framing the words, the boy asked, "Now that death has come, what does it mean? What is it that is dying? This body dies."

He lay with his limbs stretched out stiff as if rigor mortis had set in and imitated a corpse. He held his breath and felt the body silent and inert. Yet he experienced the "I" within, apart from the body. He concluded that the body dies, but the spirit that transcends it cannot be touched by death. From that moment on, the "I" or Self focused attention on itself by a powerful fascination.

Such an experience does not always result in Liberation. It may come to a seeker, but it is often lost as the inherent tendencies of the mind cloud over it. The seeker must constantly strive to purify the mind and attain complete submission so that there are no tendencies to pull him back again to the illusion of limited separate being.

In the case of the Indian boy, there was no clouding over, no relapse into ignorance. He left his

parental home without permission and found his
way to the holy Hindu mountain of Arunachala,
where he lived in silence and utter poverty. Such
was the power of his silent teaching that people
fed and clothed him. Years later he broke his silence and began to respond to questions about the
path to the Self. When his body finally died in
1950, Ramana Maharshi, addressed by the most holy
title, Bhagavan, was revered for his instruction concerning Self Inquiry as a spiritual path.

Winn Conover had never heard of Ramana
Maharshi, and yet in many ways he had died to
himself just as Maharshi had done as a boy in
South India. The process was less dramatic, more
protracted, but it had come to the unprepared Vir-
ginian nevertheless through Self Inquiry. Liberation
did not have a name or a tradition in Winn's society, but it was real. Unfortunately, it was not constant. For Maharshi, holy connection to the Divine
required no discipline. For Winn, clouds often appeared. He knew the joy of Liberation, but he had
to make a constant effort to remain free. Winn's
mind was relentless in the struggle for control. The
wars of the world are not fought over battle-scarred
terrains. They are waged moment by moment in the
minds of men. Peace is the victory of the Spirit
over the body. Winn realized this, and yet the battle
raged on. And thus every person lived out the history of the world, a history of conflict and separation. Winn was attempting to end it in the only
arena that he could.

A song sung in many churches had stated the

truth simply: "Let there be peace on earth, and let it begin with me." If the worshipers accepted the message, they did not know how to accomplish it. If they were unable to end conflict within themselves and within their own families, how could they expect the world to be different?

Winn Conover had lived with the paradox, and the conditions of living had driven him inward where he accidentally discovered Self Inquiry. But nothing occurs by accident. Winn Conover was exactly where he ought to be. Day by day, he came to accept his role, although, by his society's standards, he was a strange man in a strange land.

CHAPTER THREE

In the moments before Winn undressed and walked away from his Lakewood home, he reassured himself that his decision was rational. It may not have been realistic, but, for him at least, it was spiritually correct. He did not expect an epiphany while crossing the front lawn to the street. He did not expect to be "born again" in the manner of the fundamental Christians. He had disciplined his mind to have no expectations.

He had reasoned that when his life lost significance and yet he was capable of change, he must make the change or die inside. For when the spirit died, could the body be long in following? People did not die in the body so much as they gave up in the spirit and suffered disease. When Winn discovered that the advertised purpose of life was only material and shallow, and that his so-called achievements were meaningless, he had the choice of either slumping and then depressing himself into a coffin, or going beyond anger to find out what was important. What was real? What was true? So going naked out into the night for him was a holy pilgrimage. A pilgrimage without a destination. There was no Mecca on the horizon. The family and the police would look for a climactic emotional event, something that set him off and precipitated his departure. Ellen speculated that it was the combination of her pre-menopause, menopause, and post-menopause that had driven Winn away. She admitted that she had experienced no sexual desire for years. She had nevertheless accommodated Winn once a month despite a sometimes desperately dry vagina.

Maybe it was the dogs. Ellen had always slept with her pets. She considered relegating her darlings, always two in number, to sleeping under the bed as one of the largest sacrifices she had to make in her marriage. Winn could not abide the dogs in their bed, regardless of their size or the size of the bed. His prejudice also extended to sofas and upholstered furniture in the house. The bickering about dog hair, barking, and the relative position of canines on the evolutionary scale was a constant feature of their twenty-six-year marriage. Winn held that animals inhabiting houses as pets had rights only as assigned by their owners. The house was not the dogs' property in his opinion. Neither were dogs the equivalent of human children. Pets were to be treated with consideration and even affection, but they were not equal members of the household.

Ellen held a contradictory view about her pets. In the last six months of their marriage, both of her Pekingese had defiantly occupied the sofa in the family room as well as the pillows on Ellen's side of the bed. When Winn ceased objecting about the dogs, Ellen felt she had won a long protracted war.

The presence of the dogs in her bed also signaled the end of any sexual pressure that she felt. Winn would never attempt to be amorous while the dogs watched. There was always the possibility, too, that they might bite Winn if he attempted to mount their true master.

But it was not the dogs, or even the sex deprivation, that occupied Winn's mind in the weeks prior to this night. He was no longer at the effect of those situations. They were only elements in the mural of his past existence, and he was stepping out of that antiquated canvas. The past was static. Living was possible only in the present. The future was an absurd tense, probably invented by salesmen. When all happiness and fulfillment are projected into the future, there is no possibility for experiencing them in the now. When Winn asked himself "When do I want happiness?" the only answer was "Now."

There were several techniques that Winn had learned to keep his mind from rummaging around in the past or playing "what ifs" about the future. The mind was normally undisciplined, worse than the most impetuous child. It was in constant agitation about something or anything. Judging. Comparing. Criticizing. It had a multiple personality that could divide itself for the sake of dialogues. Winn had learned to observe these intercranial conversations as if he were an observer. Then he wondered who was the observer? And who was it that recognized the observer? Were there at least four administrators to his consciousness?

There were ways, however, to quiet the cacophony. Almost any word repeated over and over would do. Even the word "shit" would function as a mantra. The word seemed appropriate to Winn. Most of what he observed his mind thinking was shit. The process was totally unnecessary and wasteful. And the product of the undisciplined mind was garbage. Often, more nasty than garbage. It was shit. Worthless shit, unsuitable even for fertilizer.

So while the words "ow" and "ooh" involuntarily vocalized from Winn's mouth as his tender white feet encountered the edges of small rocks in the street, his mind was flooded with thought-killing mantra: "shit, shit, shit, shit . . ."

Had a lip reader encountered the overweight naked pedestrian suddenly coming out of the drizzling rain and fog into the illumination of a street light, he or she might have experienced the epiphany Winn so earnestly sought.

But no one encountered Winn as he started out of the neighborhood. Within half a block, the chill and wetness of the night caused Winn's body to shiver. The mind may have been on hold, but the instinctual nervous system sent a clear message. Winn was no yogi. He needed to cover himself.

May in Norfolk is spring-cleaning month. The trash containers at the curb, and the cardboard boxes around them, are a virtual rummage sale in an affluent neighborhood such as Lakewood. Winn was still able to say "shit" as he began to explore the contents of the trash along his path. On one curb, he found a box of castoff shoes. A pair of beat-up tennis shoes fit him. At another curb, the results of a garage clear-out yielded soiled drop cloths, brushes, worn rollers, old paint cans, and a stiff, paint-splattered pair of white overalls. The overalls were a size or two too small and required patience to squirm into, but at least they covered his nakedness. A final rummaging produced a very old and worn black sweatshirt and a dirty, baseball-style cap. The shirt had once carried the white lettering "Virginia is for Lovers" and a small heart shape painted red. The message was now unreadable without the closest inspection. The baseball-style cap was equally indistinctive. The lettering on the crown may have read "Kiss My Grits," although it was too faded for complete confirmation in the darkness.

Winn's body rejoiced as the clothed man exited the neighborhood, turned right on Lakewood Drive and then crossed the Lakewood Bridge to Granby Street. Winn stopped repeating his mantra long enough to smile. The joy had no name. It just was.

Normally, at Granby Street, you have to make a decision. If you turn right, Granby Street leads to Ocean View and the Chesapeake Bay. When Winn was a child, the Granby Street bus line ended at Ocean View Amusement Park. Local kids measured their emergence from babyhood by the first time that they rode the fearsome roller coaster at Ocean View. During Winn's childhood, the amusement park was always full of white-hatted sailors from the nearby Norfolk Naval Base. In his early teens, Trinity Baptist Church was still holding its day-long church outings under the picnic pavilion. Adjacent to the picnic area and bathhouse was a performance area where circus acts were presented. When the chimpanzee act came to the park, a kid could meet the chimps between acts and shake their hands.

In those days there were still plenty of blue crabs in the shallow bay waters that could be caught with a weighted chicken neck on a string. Winn always wanted the job of dipping the crabs as they were inch by inch brought to the surface. Once, he and his uncles and cousins had caught a bushel of big crabs in half an hour. The crabbers kept calling for Winn to dip until he had a full dozen in the net, the ones on top clawing their way to escape. Winn got ten of them to the beach and into the bushel basket. It was a great day in his childhood. Whenever he thought about Ocean View, he remembered the summer picnics, the crabbing, and the fat spot fish you could catch two at a time in late August and September. These memories did not come up when Winn approached the Granby Street traffic light this time.

If you turn left off of Lakewood Drive onto Granby Street, you immediately cross the Granby Street Bridge which breaches the main stream of the Lafayette River. The river empties into Hampton Roads near the Norfolk and Western coal piers and then carries boaters into the wide mouth of the Chesapeake Bay and into the Atlantic Ocean. Winn and his father before him had spent much of their childhood and young adult lives on these waters. There was a lingering family story about almost every point of land all the way from the Granby Street Bridge to the Atlantic Ocean.

"Here was where the outboard motor fell off the boat transom. There is where State Senator Howell, who opposed Daddy in Democratic politics, lived. There is where I learned to water ski. And these are the piers from which Uncle Joe went to World War II. Here's the place in the Bay where we watched the International Naval Review. Then we almost got swamped approaching Sandy Point when the weather turned bad. There's the beach where Granddaddy claims he caught flounder as big as a washtub. And here is where my second girlfriend, Gail, lost the top of her bathing suit in the surf."

None of these memories came up as Winn turned left and began walking along Granby Street, a route that leads directly downtown. There was no conscious decision involved. To most observers passing him, Winn resembled a street person, someone unemployed, probably destitute, maybe even dangerous. The smart thing to do, most employed people assumed, was not to make eye contact with such persons. Take a quick look, and then look away.

White people of Winn's generation would be afraid to walk down Granby Street any time of day or night. A few blocks past the bridge, the street parallels the entrances to City Park and the zoo and then makes a dog leg turn away from Church Street, the traditional Negro commercial area. During the sixties and seventies, the black population exercised its civil rights to move into the old white neighborhoods on both sides of Granby Street centered on 26th Street. A decade later, the streets were a high-crime area.

Winn's defenselessness was his safety. With no thoughts, there was no fear. With nothing to protect, he required no protection. The only objection came from Winn's body. It was not used to walking any distances. It required Winn to stop often and seek the protection of storefront doorways to get out of the rain.

There were frequent periods when Winn could relax the repetition of his mantra and observe the details of the street. At these moments, still free from the mind, he was learning to see. Free from the fragmentation caused by point of view and past experience, free from analysis, Winn experienced a new energy, a perception of totality. He was able to see without naming the object. The poverty of his surroundings became a marvelous and beautiful thing with the mind liberated from the psychological structure of society. In these moments, there was no conflict, no seeking, no asking, no desire. It was a kind of bliss.

Whenever the mind intruded into the enjoyment of seeing trees in the park lit by fog-subdued street lights, glittering in the gentle rain, Winn would quickly return to his mantra.

He would not allow his thoughts to get much beyond "I'm getting wet here. I could catch pneumonia. I should have picked a better day to be born again. Maybe I should go home."

After making the turn away from City Park, walking on the right-hand sidewalk, Winn paused to observe the old building and landscaping of the Brown & Williamson Funeral Home. Some family members of his grandfather's generation had been laid out in these funeral parlors. Before the neighborhood changed its economic class, Winn had passed this landmark more than a thousand times. It was a warm familiarity for him. He did not notice that the name on the sign had changed or that its building and grounds were far below the standards kept by Brown and Williamson. All Winn saw were the architectural lines of the stately old house and the battered high hedges exploding with tender pastel green leaves, new growth against the heavy dark background of mature green hedge.

Two blocks later, the windows of M&G Sales were fascinating in a new way. As a pre-teen, Winn and his friends had periodically disobeyed their parents and ridden their bicycles far from their suburban neighborhood to this irresistible commercial site. In the early fifties when Winn was introduced to M&G, the marine and government surplus items were still dominated by the uniforms and equipment from World War II. The proudest possessions of his childhood included a pistol belt with canteen, a helmet liner, an army haversack, and ultimately, a bayonet in its self-locking sheath.

M&G welcomed boys and allowed them to walk the narrow aisles and plunder the bins of surplus for treasure. There seemed an endless supply of items manufactured for war. They flowed in from Korea, Vietnam, and finally from the Gulf War. Boys of every generation were provided with the props for playing at soldier or sailor. Many of them would find themselves being issued similar items when

they went into military service. Being handed a real
rifle and learning to throw a real hand grenade was
a fantasy realized, although the thrill was often
short-lived.

Winn had purchased an anchor for his boat at
M&G some years before. Part of the military surplus
had given way to boating and camping goods in the
eighties. The display windows seemed better organ-
ized these days than in the heyday of the store
when inventory appeared to be placed in any space
available. Winn was conscious of none of these details, and yet the contents of the windows captured
his attention for half an hour. He viewed the artifacts like a child who, although transfixed by the
variety of shapes, could not name them or tell their
function.

CHAPTER FOUR

It was just past 4:30 A.M. when Winn disengaged himself from the display windows at M&G. Although nearly three hours had passed since he walked out his front door, he was less than two miles from home.

Ellen would sleep soundly until eight, get up leisurely, and get to the office about ten. She did not miss Winn, and she failed to notice the wallet and watch on his bureau across the room. Nor did she worry when she got the Cadillac out of her side of the garage and saw the Explorer still parked in the driveway. She assumed that a client had picked up Winn early to go look at a property or attend a breakfast meeting. She did remind herself, however, to scold Winn for forgetting to put out the trash.

Ellen would not begin to worry until after six that evening. Winn had not checked into the office, but he had failed to do so before. By 9:00 she was angry. Winn should have called if he was going to be late. Around midnight, she discovered his wallet and called her best friend. They agreed to stay calm and wait out the night. Ellen finally called the police at seven. A uniformed officer came to the house and made a report. Two days later, a detective from Missing Persons was assigned to the case.

Anyone who might have observed Winn making his slow progress up Granby Street would have labeled the man a drunk, a drug abuser, a man in shock, or a veteran of the Twilight Zone. Two police cars passed but were not motivated to stop. Perhaps the officers didn't see Winn, or they favored the dry comfort of their patrol cars to the prospect of rousting a wino.

For Winn, there was no sense of time. Each moment appeared on the loop of infinity where time and space are not even stops on life's continuous flow.

At some point beyond 26th Street, Winn drifted onto a street parallel to Granby, still headed downtown, called Monticello Avenue. He approached the Monticello Avenue underpass and walked to its bottom where the walkway provided him shelter for over an hour. His legs and feet ached. His shirt and shoes were wet. Winn did not recall the numerous times he had waited for coal trains to pass before this underpass was built. He did not appreciate the fact that he had never actually walked through the underpass before.

Up the underpass pedestrian walkway and across 21st Street appeared Doumar's, a drive-in restaurant that had survived since his parents were teenagers and came there in his father's first new car, a 1937 Model-T Ford convertible with a jump seat. Winn had brought dates to Doumar's after Granby High football games in his father's black four-door 1958 Oldsmobile. It was the first car Winn had ever seen with electric windows. Theo had dated there, too, in his father's 1985 Seville Cadillac.

In Winn's days, the waitresses roller-skated to your car in short cheerleader skirts, white blouses, and long hair ribbons that flowed down their backs and flew in the dash of their skating. The Doumar family claimed that they invented the ice cream cone, a thin waffle rolled into a cone while it was still hot and then cooled to support a huge scoop of ice cream. Winn's crowd preferred milkshakes. Ice cream cones were for kids. They took the burgers or barbecue over the hot dogs. They were also careful to count out a 10-percent tip. That was considered real sophistication.

Winn was aware that Doumar's was closed as he passed. His body would have appreciated a hot cup of coffee, but there was no opportunity and no money to pay for it.

It was just before seven when Winn approached Princess Anne Road along Monticello. Dawn had dispelled the darkness, but the overcast and still light rain made for a chilly, unwelcome morning. As Winn neared the intersection, he noticed a crowd of perhaps 100 people milling around the corner of a large auction warehouse. They seemed to be waiting for something to happen.

When he was across the street from the crowd, he could make out portable tables on the sidewalk and individuals carrying items from a van and a car parked at the curb. There was almost no traffic on the streets and very few people for blocks except for this unusual crowd. Winn crossed to see what was going on.

Most of the people milling around were men of all ages, mostly dressed for day labor. Their clothing was old and worn. Winn's attire was acceptably appropriate for the group. As he made his way, the aroma of coffee suddenly hit his nostrils like an astringent. After the initial unexpected shock, the pleasure of it settled in.

Winn leaned against the warehouse wall in an available space between two men. The small wiry black man on his left with a face full of curly white beard spoke.

"You new here, ain't you?"

"I guess I am," Winn replied with a smile. "What's going on?"

"You didn't know about the free feed?"

"No, but I sure could use a cup of coffee."

"Oh, you can get coffee, a sandwich, and bowl of hot grits, too."

"Who is doing this?"

"The Catholic Worker folks. They do this five mornings a week. They ain't with the church. The Unitarians make the sandwiches on Tuesday. But Thursday is the best day. These two fellers from St. Pius, we call 'em Bartyles and James 'cause they look like those hicks in the TV wine cooler commercials, they been coming here every Thursday for five years. Weather like this don't mean nothing to those men. They come in the snow. Instead of grits, they give you hot soup. Good soup with meat or chicken. And good sandwiches, too. Not just tuna, or peanut butter and jelly. They serve lunch meats with cheese. And they always got sweets to go with the coffee. Yes sir, you got to come early on Thursdays. I seen 130 hungry people here on a Thursday."

The black man looked more closely at Winn and then said, "You new to this thing, ain't you?"

Winn acknowledged, "How can you tell?"

"Look at your hands, man, and your face. You probably done no hard work your whole life."

"I can't remember," Winn replied.

"You ain't lost your memory, has you?"

"No, but I'm trying to," Winn said in half jest.

"I knows exactly what you mean. There's lot of stuff I wants to forget."

They both laughed.

"Where you cribbing?"

"What?"

"Where you sleep at?"

"I don't know," Winn said simply.

"On the street, uh?"

"I suppose I am."

"Well, if you got no place to go, you can talk to Steve. Them Catholic Workers don't turn down nobody. Only problem is, the way I hear it, they house is usually full of mental cases. I mean folks with serious stuff nobody else wants. Now most of the people on this street right now got mental problems. Some of these folks done time in the jacket, if you get my drift. Got to watch your step out here."

"Thank you," Winn said.

"Come on man, they beginning to serve. What's your name? My name is Bell. You know, like ding-dong."

Winn paused, not to be evasive, but to consider who he was in his new life. The question had never come up before.

"To be honest, I'm looking for a new name."

"I got you covered," Bell said with a wink. "Let's get fed and then I'll make you a deal on a Social Security card. I got your new name in my pocket."

Winn followed Bell through the line where volunteers, some Catholic, some not, greeted the nearly 100 wayfarers with warm words and smiles. Winn got his coffee with sugar, a thin tuna salad sandwich, and a paper bowl of warm instant grits. Not a grits eater, Winn followed Bell's example and put a spoonful of strawberry jam into his bowl. His mouth was delighted with the results. The hot food gave Winn's body an immediate lift. It struck him as unusual that the simple meal felt so nourishing, so invigorating.

Although the food line played to his senses, Winn had a deeper impression as he came to Steve, the Catholic Worker leader, and was served by him. Amid the activity of feeding this multitude, Steve radiated a composure, a centeredness, a compassion that Winn could feel. The closer he got to Steve, the stronger he felt it. When the grits passed into his hand, Winn looked into Steve's eyes. What was it? A healing? A forgiveness? Whatever it was, it was a powerful and special gift that Winn would use like spiritual manna in the days to come. Perhaps he would never encounter Steve again, but what was shared, wordlessly, could never be lost.

Winn and Bell found a place on the curb to eat.

"What do you know about Steve?" Winn asked.

"Oh, Steve? He was thirty last year. Has a wife and a baby. Kim, she's a Catholic Worker, too. Great guy, uh? Can you believe these people feeding us year after year? It's been six years or more. If you want to take Communion, you can get a free supper two Wednesdays a month. Not this week. Next week. But they don't try to save you. They just show up like a clock and feed us."

"What would you do if they didn't come?" Winn asked.

"Didn't come?"

"Yes. They are not part of the Catholic Church, are they?"

"No," Bell said thoughtfully.

"What happens if Steve and Kim get tired of organizing the breakfast lines and taking care of the mental cases at their shelter? What if they decide to serve God in some other way?"

"Oh, man. That would be bad. Real bad. I don't even want to think about it. This food gets us to the job. If there is no work in the labor pools, this may be all the food you gonna get that day."

"Are you going to work today?" Winn asked.

"Sure, I'm going to work. I'm going to catch me the ferry boat to Portsmouth and take the bus to the beer warehouse. They loading beer trucks twenty-four

hours a day down there. Work all you wants as
long as you wants. Five dollars a hour paid in cash.
Casual labor. No damn taxes."

"Could I get a job there, too?"

Bell raised his eyebrows. "I knows that I look
skinny and old, but I been liable to hard labor all
my life. Now you, you be lifting beer cases for a
hour and you gonna have a heart attack. They kills
people all the time at the beer warehouse. The am-
bulance carts them away and we's that's left don't
drop a case off the conveyor belt."

"I'd like to try," Winn said.

"I bet you ain't got bus fare, do you?"

"No, I don't have a cent."

"Man, you is in a terrible way. You got no
money. You got no crib. You probably got no
clothes. And you even got no name."

"That's right," Winn admitted.

"You sure is lucky that I am a God-fearing man.
Now here's what I can do. I'm taking a gamble, mind
you. But I'm willing to pay your bus fare to the beer
house and sell you my last best friend's Social Security
card. He be dead for two months and won't be need-
ing it. Then, you works for four, let's make it three
hours, on the loading line and gives me the cash and
we calls it even, bus fare and all."

"That sounds very generous to me," Winn said
nodding. "I can do three hours."

"I hopes so," Bell said getting up from the curb
and walking to a trash can.

Winn followed, noticing for the first time that the
rain had stopped and that both the Catholic Workers

and the crowd were dispersed. There were fewer
than ten people in sight. It was not yet 8:00 A.M.

"By the way," Winn asked. "What's my new
name?"

Bell turned, picking at his teeth with a fingernail.
"Your name is Booker Washington Jones."

CHAPTER FIVE

Winn Conover officially became Booker Jones when he printed the name at the top of the time card at the beer warehouse and wrote in the Social Security number. Bell was behind him when they punched in at the time clock.

"I might as well say it first. With that name and that face, everybody gonna think that your mama surely had a nigger in the woodpile."

Winn, now Booker, laughed and accompanied Bell along the long loading dock to a numbered conveyor. Soon a truck backed to the dock, and the cases of beer began to roll out to be loaded by Booker's gang of four laborers supervised by a beer distributor employee. The job was simple, but the pace of the conveyor was demanding. Sometimes there was a short break when the supervisor stopped the line to talk by hand-held intercom to someone at the warehouse end of the conveyor. It usually signaled the changeover from one type of beer to another. To Booker, however, light beer felt just as heavy as regular. There was another break when the truck was loaded and they waited for a new one to take its place.

Booker stayed the course for three hours through the morning. He had removed his cap and sweatshirt as the labor produced an intensive sweat. At times his head was giddy and light. His gloveless hands grew painfully tender in handling the abrasive beer boxes. His lower back and shoulders ached. The worst of it, however, was his crotch. Without underwear, the stiff undersized overalls were giving him an excruciating chafing.

When Booker left the line after the third hour, Bell joined him. Each man punched out and collected his wages at the cashier's window. Then they went to rest in a break room that consisted of bare six-foot tables, metal folding chairs, and a row of vending machines against one wall. A water fountain and bathroom were along the wall just outside. Five men were already in the room when they arrived. Three of them were asleep in the chairs, their heads resting on folded arms.

Hard physical labor seems to focus the mind on the task, thus releasing the consciousness for a time from its normal fragmented chatter. Repetitive efforts, like the repetitive mantra, keep the mind occupied in a non-destructive pattern. What is perhaps taxing to the body becomes relaxation to the mind. Very little came into Booker's mind while he was struggling with the beer cases. His total attention was focused on the job. So while his body experienced damage, Booker's mind experienced a kind of joy. Office workers experience this joy in gardening. Prisoners have experienced this joy in breaking rocks. The fragmentation of the mind can be overcome in work.

Booker handed over his pay to Bell as agreed. Then Bell found change to buy each of them a soft drink.

"You'd think with all the beer they got laying around here, they'd let you have a cold one in the break room," Bell remarked as he handed Booker the drink.

The men took seats opposite each other and enjoyed the first taste of beverage.

"What you going to do now?" Bell asked.

"I might take a nap and then go back on the line. If I didn't hurt so much, I'd think I enjoyed it."

"You better like it if you gonna get out of your fix, man," Bell advised. "You know how many cases you got to carry to buy one pair of pants? How many you got to move to sleep someplace decent tonight? When you starts with nothing every morning, you got to work like this just to get by."

Booker's mind flickered into the memories of Winn. He held his breath in an attempt to freeze the unwanted retrogression. Images re-emerged when he took the next inhalation, so he fell back on his mantra.

"Shit is right, man," Bell observed. "No matter how many times you say it. Life is shit, and we are the factories. We're shit factories, plain and simple."

Booker had to laugh. "I wasn't saying shit to comment," he said in an attempt to explain. "I said shit in order to focus."

Bell looked at him oddly.

"Whatever," he said and let it go. He had had too many unintelligible conversations with deranged street people to question anyone's logic. "I'm going to do me another two hours and get back to Norfolk. I helps a restaurant cook take out the night garbage, so he saves me the pick of what comes back on the plates. It's more than I can eat, so I take a bag over to one of the old-timers living downtown on Social Security. They live in crummy little rooms, but at least I can trade the food for a night on the floor. That's how I come to have your Social Security card. I woke up one morning, and my main man was dead."

"You did him a great service by bringing him the food," Booker observed.

"We have to take care of each other, don't we?" Bell reasoned. "When the old-timers get sick and can't leave their rooms, or the cops come and take away their hot plates, how they gonna eat?"

Bell drained his drink and prepared to go back to work.

"I hope old Booker has a more better life the second time around than he had the first time. Poor boy killed himself with alcohol. I hope you do good by his name. Just don't tell nobody how you come by it."

Booker stood and extended his hand. "I'm very grateful to you for your help."

Bell took the hand, but seemed embarrassed by the sentiment and avoided the other man's eyes.

"Just pass it along. That's all we can do."

When Booker went back on the line, he did not

see Bell. There were four conveyors working that day and a lot of activity on the loading dock. Bell was used to meeting other indigent men. He was a talker, and there were always five or more new people passing through Norfolk who turned up for a Catholic Worker breakfast. The man, now called Booker, was just another encounter, albeit a profitable encounter, for Bell. To Booker, however, it was the first friendship of his new life. Winn had never had a black friend. Bell had been a completely new experience. Bell had trusted him, had helped him. Would Winn have done the same? No, not as Winn. Not for a black street person. But now, as Booker, he wanted to further extend his heart and his hand to Bell. But Bell was gone, and Booker missed him. All Booker could do was to send a blessing of gratitude to Bell. It was a silent blessing that went forth whenever he remembered.

Booker stayed on the line only two hours before he had to take a break. He ate a meal of peanut butter crackers and a carton of milk from the vending machines and then slept almost two hours slumped over a table in the break room. Then he went back to the line. It was the only thing he knew to do. The pattern continued throughout the night.

During a long break late into the night, Booker sat with his baseball cap in hand, turning it without purpose. His eyes came to focus on its weathered peak where only a faint outline of what had been lettering remained. The eyes, used to "for sale" signage, wanted to organize the obscure patterns into words. The mind involuntarily recognized the three stacked symbols as EAT MY GRITS. Booker then awoke to their significance.

Winn was never a believer in supernatural magic. Fortune tellers, occultists, clairvoyants, and their ilk were tricksters in his opinion. Reality was mathematical, predictable. Miracles could be explained as cause and effect if all the elements could be examined. This, Winn believed, was the power of rational intellect. It could, or would, ultimately explain everything. But here, coming into focus, was something mystical: the randomness of a discarded cap, a message almost totally obscured, a connection to something divine. The cap proclaimed EAT MY GRITS, and then the reborn man is served a meal of grits from the hands of a saint. That's how Booker recalled his encounter with Steve, the Catholic Worker.

Booker now saw the message on the cap as an instruction. EAT MY GRITS really meant RECEIVE MY MANNA. The grits were a communion food. The miracle to Booker meant that he was on the correct path. The connection between the cap and the charity of his first meal could not be a coincidence. Its relevance seemed very clear to him.

Booker could not avoid thinking, but he was very disciplined not to revert to Winn's experience. He asked himself some basic questions about the separation.

Is it possible to live without memories? Is it possible to relate to another human being without talking about the past? Who we think we are is so dependent on the past. Who was Winn-Booker if he could not say that he had an MBA from UVA? How could he define himself without referring to his resumé of accomplishments? He was in real estate. He was married over twenty-five years, with two grown children. He was raised a Baptist. He was a president of his Kiwanis Club.

But Bell had not asked his pedigree. Bell had imposed no requirements on friendship. Perhaps the real equality between people could be enjoyed only at the lowest rung of society where there was little to gain or lose. In that environment, giving often seemed the same as receiving.

By seven that morning, Booker was exhausted. Since he had last seen Bell, he had worked ten hours and collected fifty dollars. Shift workers at the warehouse were leaving the building for the employee parking lot. Booker approached several of the men before he secured a ride.

"I can drop you off at the truck stop on Route 58," one of them offered for the consideration of two dollars. At the end of the ride, however, the man refused the money. "You'd do better to spend it on a shower," he suggested.

Truck stops not only have showers, but also have general stores for the convenience of the truckers. Booker purchased a new lightweight pair of overalls in his size, underwear, socks, tee shirt, toothbrush, toothpaste, a bar of soap, a comb, and a small jar of Vaseline. When he paid at the section reserved for professional drivers and asked for a shower and a rack to sleep in, the manager did not question him.

That afternoon when he awoke, he dressed out clean but unshaven and carried his belongings in a plastic retail bag to the truck stop restaurant. He spent all but two dollars remaining from his wages on a meal of eggs, biscuits, coffee, and, of course, grits.

By four that afternoon, after asking six drivers if they needed unloading help, Booker secured a ride with a trucker headed for Greensboro, North Carolina.

"You won't be talking my head off, will you?" the driver asked. "I don't mind giving you a ride. I just don't want to hear no life stories."

"That's fine with me," Booker agreed.

CHAPTER SIX

The ride to Greensboro was filled with country music tapes played against a background of conversations on the CB radio. The driver of the United moving van finally turned the music off to use the radio for local directions to a neighborhood where he was to unload his cargo of furniture and household goods. After more than four hours on the road, he spoke to Booker for the first time since they had settled into the cab of the Peterbilt 372.

"How long you been a lumper?"

"Been a what?" Booker asked.

"A lumper. I figured you for a lumper when you asked me for a job at the truck stop."

"I'm new at this kind of work," Booker admitted.

"Well, I guess you are. If I wasn't running late, I'd have tried to pick up some casual labor off the street, or called one of the agencies. But they would all be closed by the time we got here. This load is promised for today, no matter if we have to unload it at midnight."

"I'm glad to help," Booker responded.

"Tell you what. You do a good job and hold up your end till we get it done, and I'll pay you ten dollars an hour from the time we park till the time we pull ole Peterbilt away from the house. What do you say?"

"That sounds good to me. Will that make me a lumper?"

"I guess it will. I'll drop you off at a truck stop on I-40 when we're through. You can get a bunk and then maybe get another job tomorrow."

"Is that what lumpers do?" Booker asked.

"Sure. Lumpers hang around truck stops and ware-houses looking for a job. The trucking companies can't afford to pay helpers to go on the road, so they give drivers a cash allowance to hire help on the delivery end. If you are driving a moving van, you got to find a helper or ruin yourself trying to do the job single-handed. It's a pain in the ass to have to look for a helper in a strange town. In some places, it can be downright dangerous. You don't know who you are taking into your rig. Most likely it's some wino who can't support his end of a sofa and light-loads you all day long, or it's some character with an attitude who pisses off the cus-tomers and gets you in trouble. I didn't smell no liquor on you, you had all your teeth, and you talked good, so I took a chance. I know some reg-ular lumpers, and I use them whenever I can. A dependable lumper is a truck driver's friend. You do me right, and I'll pass the word to the other drivers. You can always work if you want to."

"And they will let me travel with them?" Booker asked.

"Well, they probably won't let you bed down with

them in the sleeper, but if you pay your own meals and such, most drivers will give you a long ride. Some lumpers follow the sun like gypsies. It's a pretty good trick if you think about it. Everything paid in cash. No taxes. No address where people can find you."

"Yes," Booker pondered. "Of course, you could never own more than you could carry."

The job that night lasted well past midnight. When the dining room table and chairs were carried into the house, the customers set out a picnic buffet to share with the movers. Booker worked hard, struggling at times on the front steps and on the stairs to the second floor with mattresses, triple dressers, and heavy chests of drawers. Jim, the driver, coached his lumper on how to use his legs in lifting rather than his back. Booker also learned how to use an appliance dolly.

When the van was empty and all the beds were set up, the customers released the tired driver and his gentle but exhausted older helper. The man of the family pressed a twenty-dollar tip on Booker in a sincere handshake of gratitude. Later, Jim rounded off the hours of work with another fifty dollars.

Booker left Jim in the truck stop parking lot where the driver planned to bunk in his rig's sleeper before going back to the road. As he paid for his own bunk in the drivers' dormitory, Booker smiled with satisfaction. He was self-sufficient. He had found a way to live. He was a lumper.

The next morning, however, Booker was not sure that he could remain a lumper. During the night, he was awakened twice with searing cramps in both calves. He bolted upright in bed, massaged the over-worked muscles, and then arched his toes to stretch them into relief. When he got out of bed to go to the toilet, he tottered like an octogenarian in need of an aluminum walker. Every movement made him believe that his limbs would crack like plaster and leave him a less-than-white marble Greek torso on the floor. Booker wore a body suit of pain, awful, binding pain that would not allow his arms to raise high enough to brush his teeth. Combing his hair was completely out of the question even after he had stood under a very hot shower for twenty min-utes. His movement was so restricted that he could not use the soap. There was nowhere on his body that he could reach.

Booker invested in a bottle of aspirin and another day of rest at the truck stop. He made it to the restaurant twice, but spent most of the twenty-four hours in bed. The next day, feeling better, he walked to a manufacturers outlet shopping center on the other side of the interstate and purchased a pair of leather work shoes, a light jacket, a pair of work gloves, and a cheap nylon backpack to carry his be-longings.

Getting a ride and a job was much easier now that Booker knew the routine. At the gas pumps and com-ing from the restaurant he looked for a driver who was driving a moving van. His approach was straight-forward, like a man who knew his business.

"Hi, my name is Booker Jones. Do you need a lumper today? I'm looking for a ride west."

The driver put out his cigarette and eyeballed the older man with the prickly white beard. The man was overweight, but he seemed fit. His eyes were bright and clear. No signs of drug or alcohol abuse.

"I might need some help. When was your last job?" the driver asked to qualify.

"I did a load with Slim Jim, the United driver, in Greensboro day before yesterday," Booker replied without hesitation.

"OK," the driver considered, "but I'm not unloading in Memphis until tomorrow."

"That's fine," Booker assured him. "I can eat and sleep in a truck stop at your convenience. You just tell me when to go and when to come back to the truck."

The driver liked the sound of what Booker was saying. Obviously the man knew the rules of the game and was not going to try to con him out of meals and a snooze in his sleeper. Then, too, if the man proved to be a problem, he could always send him into the truck stop for cigarettes and leave his ass behind anywhere along the route. Having a lumper on board, however, would make the turn-around in Memphis a lot easier.

"OK. What did you say your name was?"

"Booker."

"OK, Booker. You got yourself a ride. The job at the end will take about four or five hours, depending on the house. The pay is twelve dollars an hour, top wages for a helper who knows what he is doing."

"I can hold up my end," Booker replied as he offered his hand.

The driver laughed as he shook hands. "You are about as mannered a lumper as I ever met."

"I'm from the old school, the real old school," Booker jested as he stroked his white beard for emphasis.

"I think I'll call you Uncle Booker," the good-natured driver said. "My name is Johnny. My handle is Little John. Let's ride."

Riding shotgun in a big sixteen wheeler like Little John's 400-horsepower Kenworth truck was like being enclosed in a vibrating cocoon. Once the shifting of gears was completed and the rig was on the interstate highway, the roar of the engine became a steady drone. The height of the cab gave a clear view of the road ahead, but if you relaxed in the seat, none of the passing traffic was visible or could be heard. In some ways, the speeding truck seemed almost like a spaceship. Although the truck traveled hundreds of miles, the passenger hardly moved at all. Destinations were mere places in time. The truck went on and on. The passenger exited at will to enter the temporal world.

Booker learned to use the rhythm of the road as a meditation. The simple act of intently watching his mind brought it to silence. The process was a gradual withdrawal. The watched mind yielded to fewer and fewer thoughts until it was quiet. Booker began to recognize this state by the feeling of fullness in the right side of his chest. When he was no longer living in his mind, it did not matter if his eyes were open or closed. He was completely sentient, but the awareness was nameless, undisturbing.

In this state, Booker could respond to Little John's questions without disruption. Time was effortless. Because he was at peace, the projected lower lip and the odd facial mannerism which had characterized Winn to his friends and family were absent. His face, free from fragmented thought, was totally relaxed. At night when Booker slept, he experienced a dreamless sleep that was totally refreshing. Booker did not constantly turn in the bed to seek comfort. He did not sweat or wake up three or four times a night without apparent reason as Winn had done for years.

Without emotional stress, the body carried out its own healing. Booker's body, which had endured intense, punishing labor, was rebounding in a way Winn's body could never have been expected to perform. The foods provided were metabolized differently. The blood pressure and the heart rate cooperated in a new alignment of functional priorities. Even the libido lessened its demands.

Into the fourth day of his rebirth, the new man had no desire to know the world news or to anticipate the weather. He asked only the questions required by the function. He responded only in the present. And yet he was no automaton. He recognized humor and was open to laughter. He was spontaneous, but the behavior translated as consideration, even kindness.

Most of the lumpers that drivers met and worked with were unhappy men, forced into itinerant labor by failure and lack of resources. Whatever confidence or humor they displayed was too often superficial.

They could turn sullen and argumentative with the slightest provocation. Too many of them drank excessively or used drugs. They could be mean and unpredictable. A driver was seldom at ease around a lumper, especially one who was a stranger.

Booker was different. It was not definable to the drivers, not in ways that they could articulate, but this man was easy to be around. Someone into occult images might have said that Booker had a good aura or that he gave off positive vibes. Whatever the name, it was a welcomed attribute on a dangerous road that drivers had to face every day.

Winn Conover was not dead. A foreign entity had not inhabited his body and destroyed his memories. When Booker looked into a mirror, he saw both Winn and Winn's father. There was a warmth there that represented forgiveness. Winn's father died in late 1993. Their relationship contained love and respect, but there always seemed a barrier to expressing it. Their life together seemed one long debate about politics, crime, welfare, war. They were seldom silent around each other, the void always demanding talk. Now Booker could speak for both men, reconciling them to their true affection for each other. There could be peace and closure. It was a matter of choice. Booker chose for Winn. He chose love over fear. He chose forgiveness over guilt.

The tableau of Winn's memory was a library. Booker had the library card. He could choose what books to open and what books to leave closed. Winn had never had that conscious choice. Booker also realized that he could edit and even rewrite

Winn's collection of books as he had rewritten
Winn's unfulfilled relationship with his deceased father. Booker made the book have a happy ending.
Winn and his father were finally able to say "I love
you."

When Winn's troubled memories came up in
Booker's awareness, he no longer attempted to beat
them down with the mantra. Rather, he unraveled
them, remade them, healed them and allowed them
to evaporate into nothingness, never to be important
again. This process is what spiritual seekers refer to
as *working on yourself*. During the ride to Memphis,
Booker experienced periods of complete bliss. Whenever Winn's old thought system broke into consciousness, Booker gently brought it to the light of
the new awareness, and it lost its power. This was
the freedom Winn had sought and Booker had ob-
tained. But the freedom required constant vigilance.
It was a discipline that demanded practice. Booker
internalized the idea as "I must always remember
who I am." In the days to come, his resolve would
be severely tested. The world had a consistent history of murdering its saints.

CHAPTER SEVEN

The ride to Memphis with a few stops took fourteen hours. It was after midnight when Little John exited the interstate, turned away from the truck stop, and continued a mile farther down the intersecting road to a poorly lit, nondescript, rectangular building surrounded by a gravel parking lot.

"I'm going to stop for a few beers to unwind. If there are some women in there, maybe I'll get lucky. You can come on in or walk back to the truck stop and I'll meet you in the morning."

"I'll come in," Booker replied.

Unlike Johnny, who was road weary, Booker was awake and alert. If the driver had impressed on him that they had traveled over 650 miles, he would have marveled at the passage. His mind could not account for the time because it had been occupied so little.

Booker could hear the loud revelry before they got to the door, then a blast of music, human voices, colored lights, and the smell of cigarettes, beer, and sweat assaulted them as they entered. Although Saturday night had recently turned into Sunday morning, the party continued for about seventy working class patrons.

The bar started at the door and ran the entirety of one wall. Most of its seats were taken by casually dressed men and women in western-style shirts and jeans. Some of the men had their hats on. There were two styles: baseball caps or wide-brimmed cowboy hats. Two thirds of the room was occupied by tables and booths along two walls. A small stage and dance floor was at the far end of the room. The ceiling seemed low, as if to compress the power of the music and drinks. A four-piece pop country band was into its final performance set. Most of those with partners were dancing.

Although there are thousands of country music bars in the United States where blue-collar people go for entertainment and relaxation, none of them was included in Winn's library of experiences.

Johnny went directly to the bar and ordered a beer. Booker followed and when the bartender asked for his order, he surprised himself by saying, "Orange juice and ginger ale, half and half, please."

"With vodka?" the barman questioned.

"No, thanks."

"What kind of drink is that?" Johnny asked.

"I don't know," Booker smiled. "I never had it before."

"Uncle Booker, you are a strange dude. Come on, man, loosen up. Have some fun. We've got to hump our asses off tomorrow, so let's get loose."

"I'm loose," Booker assured him.

Johnny left the bar and began to look for friends among the tables. Booker enjoyed his drink and began to absorb the strange new territory. The dancing was especially interesting to watch. There were couples who seemed to be doing an old-fashioned two-step mixed in with elaborate spins and twirls of the female partner. They seemed to be following an oval on the dance floor the way ballroom couples did in the days of full gowns and Viennese waltzes. But what fascinated Booker was the uncoupled dancers who seemed to be in lines. They were synchronous! He had to get closer to confirm his observation, so he went to the edge of the dance floor where the line dancers were performing.

He had finished his drink and was watching the line dancers into a third tune, when one of them, a stout woman over forty, pulled him onto the floor and encouraged him to follow her and learn the steps. Booker was amazed at how quickly his feet mimicked the dance. The steps were not complex, a basic pattern mixed with simple turns or spins. All the years Winn had devoted to party dancing while in high school and college were remembered by Booker's feet. Within two dances, Booker was a part of the line, picking up quickly any variations when the music changed.

"You are a natural, Honey," the woman who had been his instructor observed.

Booker was too given to the moment of dancing in synchronization to consider how ridiculous and self-conscious his activity would have seemed to Winn. Being lured onto a dance floor by an unappealing stranger where you could possibly humiliate yourself would have been an impossible act for

Winn. With no investment in an image, Booker, however, was free to experience the fun.

Over the music, the woman, Janice, invited Booker to waltz. She explained that she was a widow and had come to the club with her sister and brother-in-law. Looking at Booker's overalls, she asked, "You come right from work, Honey? You on the night shift?"

"No, actually, I came in right off the truck," Booker explained.

"Right off the truck!" Janice howled with laughter. "That's a good one."

Booker and Janice were moving enthusiastically around the dance oval when the commotion began. Two men were struggling in each other's grasp, each trying to keep the other from using his fists. Chairs were being overturned and tables moved so violently that bottles and glasses were breaking on the floor. Other patrons around them scurried to get out of their way. From his place on the dance floor, Booker recognized one of the men as Johnny. The other man was much larger than Johnny and seemed to be the more angry and aggressive of the pair. He was making it clear to Johnny and to everyone else in the place who could hear that he intended to rip Little John's head off.

Booker left his dance partner and walked through the circle of onlookers to the fighting pair.

"Brother, Brother, do you need any help?" Booker asked when he got close to them.

"You're damn right I need help," Johnny screamed. "Get this bastard off me."

"I wasn't talking to you, sir," Booker replied. He looked the other man in the eyes. "I was talking to you, Brother."

"You ain't my brother," the big man spit out as he attempted to gain advantage on Johnny.

"Of course I'm your brother. Don't you recognize me? I've been looking for you for years. We have the same Father."

"You're nuts," the man grunted.

"Hit him," Johnny shouted.

"What's happened to make you feel this way?" Booker pleaded to the man, ignoring Johnny.

"What's happened? What's happened?" the man asked in disbelief. "You asshole, everything has happened."

"We need to talk," Booker said simply.

"Go to hell!" the man said with bitterness as he wrestled with Johnny.

"Come on. Think. Who is more important? This man you are fighting or me, your own brother who has come to help you?"

"You ain't my brother."

"I am your brother, and I can prove it. Let this man go so we can talk. If I am not your brother, you can beat on me."

The man stopped struggling with Johnny, who slumped against his huge chest.

"Let him go," Booker said gently. "What we have to do is more important."

"If I let this bastard go, and you ain't my brother, I'll kill you. I swear."

"OK. That's a deal."

The man looked into Booker's face then down to the bald spot on the crown of Johnny's head. He pushed the smaller man away. Johnny did not resist and landed seat first on the floor.

As the crowd converged around the men, Booker offered a hand and helped Johnny to his feet.

"What's his name?" Booker asked.

"Bob Wilson. Bad Bobby Wilson. Let's get the hell out of here," Johnny whispered.

"Let me talk to Bob. I'll meet you at the truck."

"Are you nuts? You pulled it off. Now let's run."

Booker did not respond, but stepped around Johnny and walked directly to Bob Wilson. Johnny used the opportunity to move back into the crowd and make a circuitous exit to his truck. He watched the front door in anticipation of the momentary ejection of Uncle Booker's inert body.

Inside, the band had used the fight as its cue to quit for the night. People began leaving and two waitresses were already beginning to clean up the broken glass and to restore the tables and chairs to normality.

Bob Wilson spoke to the people at his table and then motioned Booker to a table where they could sit alone.

"So you are my long lost brother?" Wilson began with a sneer and demand. "What's your name?"

"Booker Jones."

"OK. Start explaining. And it better be good 'cause I am still drunk, I am still big, and I am still mean."

"You said everything had happened when I asked

you why you were so upset. What exactly is trou-
bling you? I know it's not that truck driver. It must
be something serious." Booker's tone was even and
calm. His eyes offered contact to the other man.

"It's serious enough if you consider divorce and losing your job serious." Wilson's tone was less defiant.

"Bob, I didn't know. You must be in a lot of
pain."

"You're damn right I am."

"But you can't show it to anyone, can you?"

"No, you can't show it. They will think that you
are a loser."

"You are not a loser, Bob. I can see that. You
just need to put things into their proper place. It's
all going to work out for you."

"Maybe. I don't know. Betty is going to move
back to Ohio with the kids. I've fucked up just like
my father—the booze, the fighting . . ."

"That can all be corrected," Booker reassured. "You
made some errors, but they can be made right."

"How the hell can you do that?"

"You have to forgive yourself. You have to love
yourself."

"Are you some kind of preacher?" Wilson asked
defensively. "I already been saved four or five times.
It don't do me no good."

"Bob, I'm just like you. I've got the same struggle.
Let me show you a couple of things that have
helped me."

"Where you gonna show me?"

"Right here. Right now. Brother to brother. We
can do it in five minutes."

"So show me."

"First we have to learn a new way to breathe."

"You're kidding. Breathing is going to solve my problems?"

"Yes, it's the first step. Trust me."

In the next minutes, Booker showed Bob Wilson how to control his breathing and focus his mind. The exercise was very relaxing. It lowered Wilson's heart rate and respiration and changed the rigid expression on his face.

"Get to that place where your mind is quiet and then listen for the voice that will guide you," Booker concluded. "That's all you have to do."

"Do that and I get a job?" Bob asked.

"Yes," Booker affirmed.

"Do that and Betty comes back to me."

"Yes, even that is possible. Just make sure that you are in the quiet place whenever you talk to her."

"So I won't yell and cuss her?"

"Exactly."

"OK. Now tell me how you are my brother." Bob was relaxed, but earnest.

"Stay with your breathing to hear this," Booker advised. "Listen for the voice to tell you if it is true."

"OK," Wilson agreed.

"All men on this planet can trace their genes to only two females. There are only two biological mothers of us all. Since you and I are from the same race, we had the same mother. This is scientifically correct. Now the Father who gave you life also gave it to me. He is the voice that we hear in the silence. He leads us to what is true and good for us. We are His sons. And as His sons, you and I are brothers."

"I'm a little confused," Bob admitted.

"I was confused for fifty-four years," Booker said as he laid his hand on Bob's. "It takes practice to hear our Father. Don't be discouraged. Go to Him in the quiet of your mind, and He will tell you what you need to know. He will tell you that I am absolutely your own dear brother."

"I don't know what to say," Bob said. "I know you ain't a queer, and you ain't trying to sell me anything. So, in a crazy way, you might be right."

"Does that mean I can go without you trying to kill me?"

Both men laughed.

"I've got a ride waiting," Booker said.

"Yeah, me too. You want to get together later?" Bob asked.

"I'm on the road," Booker explained. "You don't need me specifically. Just look around. You've got a billion brothers to keep you company."

"I hope I see you again," Bob said, offering a handshake.

"Me too," Booker agreed.

"I'm glad you stopped me from hurting Little John. I been knowing that guy for ten years."

"What was the problem?"

"We lost track of who was buying the rounds. I don't need much of an excuse lately. I wasn't really beating up on Johnny. I was just beating up on my-self again."

"You got it, Bob. That's the kind of truth you get in the quiet place."

"I see what you mean. Thanks, Brother."

When Booker climbed back into the cab of the Kenworth, Johnny was exuberant.

"I don't see any blood. What happened? What took you so long to get away?"

"I had to convince Bob that I was his brother."

"And he bought it?"

"Yes, I guess he did."

"Unbelievable!"

"Look him up next time you are down here. He probably wants to apologize to you."

"Oh brother! I can't believe it," Johnny exclaimed. "I owe you one. Really. I could have gotten hurt in there. They don't call him Bad Bobby for nothing."

"He might have to change his name, too," Booker said as an aside.

"What?"

"Nothing. Can we get back to the truck stop? We've got a big day tomorrow. You could use the rest."

"Sure," Johnny said. "Let's meet in the restaurant about nine for breakfast. I'm buying."

The memory of Winn Conover could not recall intervening into the personal life of anyone outside his immediate family. Even as a teenager, Winn would never have considered breaking up a fist fight. If people wanted to fight, let them. He took no responsibility for other people's stupidity or for their anger. Thus, there was no precedent when Booker acted in the case of Little John vs. Bad Bobby.

Sharing a truck ride is not like crossing the ocean with shipmates. There is not the kind of bonding that makes complete strangers, united only by the name of a ship, defend each other in barroom brawls. Booker had not acted out of truck-board loyalty to Johnny. Looking back at the event, which he did not do, Booker would not have found a definable motivation. Like the spontaneity of learning to line dance, Booker was disjointed from cause and effect. If action can be said to be pure, this was pure, uncaused action.

Booker had no plan as he approached the two struggling men. He did not touch them. He did not posture around them like a ring referee. He had no idea why he called the total stranger "brother." And upon that opening, he had no scenario of where it might lead. So how was he to explain what transpired to Little John or to anyone else for that matter? Booker could not accept the credit for averting disaster, a credit Johnny so lavishly wanted to bestow, because he, Booker, had not been the doer.

All day long as they moved furniture out of the van, Johnny wanted to replay the events of the previous night. Booker, however, was content with the activity of the move-in itself. His body, recovered from the Greensboro job, was fit for the work. There was joy in the flexing of the muscles and in the oily sweat that seemed to wash away the excess of a sedentary lifestyle. Each new object in the move was treasure recovered from the depths of the van and brought into the light, restored to its function. As the empty house filled with the elements of the family's life, Booker could feel their elation. He was with them in solidarity for the love and comfort that the house-become-home represented. He could sense the growth of this feeling as the van emptied.

When Johnny wanted to talk about the previous night, Booker would turn on the question like a ballerina en pirouette and rhapsodize on the virtues of being a mover.

"This is a great job," Booker said as Johnny contemplated how to get an upright piano into the family room. "These people trust us to get everything that they own to this destination. And then we get to see and touch all the personal stuff of their environment. It's so fascinating."

"Trust me," Johnny warned. "It's not so fascinating the fourth or fifth time. By the time you get to a hundred, you wouldn't care if you were moving Princess Di out of Buckingham Palace."

At another time when Johnny persisted, Booker turned his attention to the day, although he did not recognize it as a Sunday.

"Look at that sky, Johnny. What a day to be working outside. And those azaleas in the beds against the house. Aren't they perfect?"

Uncle Booker usually didn't talk unless someone asked him a question. Yet Booker was a pleasure to have on the job. His focus was always on the task, and he worked well without supervision. Johnny thought he would have to pace the old boy to get him through the load, but it was Johnny who called for the breaks.

When the job was over and Johnny returned Booker to the interstate truck stop, he found it hard to leave the lumper behind. Along with a generous payoff of $75, Johnny gave Booker a handwritten reference on van line stationery.

"Booker Jones is a first class lumper. He is clean and sober. He works hard and knows how to handle furniture. Customers like him. He is a fine man who is very loyal. I trust and respect Booker Jones. Any truckers who work with him will find him a friend."

CHAPTER EIGHT

Booker got a job Monday morning on a moving van only two hours away from its delivery address in Little Rock, Arkansas. The trucker, who was already three days out of Washington, D.C., was glad to get a lumper. Booker didn't need to use the reference letter Little John had given him the night before.

The driver was a well-spoken black man whose CB handle was Alley Cat.

"That's Mr. Alley Cat to you," he advised Booker.

On the ride to Little Rock, Alley Cat, a man of forty who could look distinguished in a well-fitting suit, asked Booker's full name and lumper experience.

"Let me get his straight. Your full name is Booker Washington Jones?"

"That's right," Booker replied.

"How in the world did you get a name like that?"

Booker answered flatly for effect. "I've been told that my mother might have had someone lurking in the woodpile."

There was a brief but obvious pause, and then Alley Cat erupted. He pounded the wheel with the

palm of his right hand and laughed until tears involuntarily filled his eyes.

"You are all right, Booker Washington Jones. It is
always nice to have a brother on the job. My name
is Cliff Williams."

Williams held his right hand in the air. Booker
was confused for a second and then realized what
to do. Winn had watched enough sports television
to know the gesture. Booker turned slightly and
slapped Williams' raised hand with his own right
hand. The high-five was both a greeting and a celebration.

The customers were moving into an affluent Little
Rock neighborhood. The house was substantial, and
the couple who awaited them were probably not yet
forty, well-groomed and well-spoken. They looked
like they might be college faculty or professional
careerists. They had no children.

In the process of handling the customer's belongings, a good driver and his lumper need to establish
a quick rapport with the individuals. Trust and confidence mixed with cooperation and consideration go
a long way in making the move-in a happy, if la-
borious, experience.

The exchange of first names is a beginning which
leads to coordination in the work and, over the
hours, perhaps a meal together and then a sense of
familiarity. It is a surprisingly rapid process for
strangers to make, but it often happens when people work together on a common goal such as moving furniture into an empty house and thereby
transforming it into a new home. Familiarity leads

to conversation and sometimes revelation. Exposition is more common than confession, but the content, like advice, is offered sincerely.

Paul and his wife Zena were refugees from the Clinton presidential administration. Although they were pleasant and even friendly to Cliff and Booker, there was an undercurrent of bitterness about their return to Little Rock.

What Paul would not tell the news media, he would say to two common working men whom he had hoped to help by his service in the national government. Perhaps telling them about his experience was an apology for failure.

As the bed was being set up in the final bedroom, Paul tried to summarize the running conversation that he had begun with a shared lunch.

"Nobody in government, especially the Congress, means what he says," Paul complained. "All the promises are nothing but rhetoric designed for the media. Behind the images are selfish people doing what is best for themselves. A president, any president, steps on the Washington stage, and it immediately tilts, throwing him off balance. Then he stays off balance. Special interests playing to private greed is the best description of how we are governed. Whoever comes into that system is either corrupted or eliminated.

"I went to Washington believing that good people working together could make changes and solve problems. Having seen the people in power, I know that it is impossible. From Congressional leaders to the lowest bureaucrat, no one will accept responsibility for what is stupid, what is excessive, or what is corrupt. The finger of blame is never pointed at themselves.

"I went to Washington as a democratic activist. I return home as a revolutionary. Let's get rid of the bastards."

"Honey," Zena said to console him. "We're not cut out to be radicals."

"What else is there left to be?" he responded in a hopeless voice.

"It's not your fault," Cliff offered. "I've been moving these people in and out of Washington for twenty years. Congressmen arrive with half a load of ordinary goods, and they retire with vans full of treasure. They sell us out. Look at the streets of the District. They have to see the crime, the violence, and the poverty all around them. They are either blind or they just don't give a damn as long as they are on top."

"You haven't said much, Booker," Zena observed. "You probably have more right to be angry than any of us."

In the memory of Winn's experience, there were many negative attitudes about excessive government and corrupt politics. Winn could recall when his father's political friends purchased black votes with bags of five dollar bills on Norfolk's Church Street. He had witnessed U.S. Senate seats from Virginia going to fools and then to men he judged to be immoral and unethical. Winn Conover had volumes of opinions and anecdotes to contribute on the decline of America. He knew too well the fortunes made by local politicians in manipulative land deals. He knew about the payoffs and the ole boy networks. What he ultimately knew was that the members of Congress reflected exactly what the rest of the country was like. Free enterprise was a polite cover name for naked materialism. Democracy had become another name for arrogant paternalism. But these were Winn's ideas, and Booker did not choose to use them.

"I'm not angry," Booker began. "Working to be self-sufficient seems reasonable to me. I've found that society is made up of individuals. At the individual level, you can see constant examples of unselfishness and kindness. A smile given to a stranger can be an important gift. It changes arrogance into compassion. The test of our country is not the power of our institutions, but how much we trust each other as individuals. Government is not the problem. The problem, as I see it, is relationships. Husbands with wives. Parents with children. Neighbors with other neighbors. And finally, strangers with strangers."

There was a long silence after Booker spoke. Then Paul asked, "How can you afford to be so generous? Are you a rich man or a priest masquerading as a laborer?"

"No," Booker laughed. "I think my net worth is about eighty dollars in cash and clothes enough to fill a small backpack."

"But you are educated," Zena remarked.

"That may be subject to debate. But education and intellect do not teach us the things we really need to know. How can we relate to each other through concepts? Cliff is a truck driver. You and Paul are administrators. I am a laborer. Is that who we really are? Do we get together socially for intimate dinners to find out?"

"We did today," Paul said. "It may have been fried chicken from a take-out, but we got together."

"Yes, we did," Booker said. "That's what I love about the moving business. You get to work on new relationships every day."

"This brother is strange," Cliff said with pride. "He talks like a preacher and works like a stevedore."

The need to complete the work precluded extending the conversation, and the four individuals returned to their respective tasks. When the moving manifest was ready to be signed, and the farewells were being said, Zena slipped thirty dollars into Booker's hand.

"We're grateful to you, Booker," she said. "Both Paul and I needed to hear what you said upstairs. We are coming off a bad experience. We need a new point of view, both professionally and personally. I think you helped us to find it."

It was late in the afternoon when Cliff went out of his way to drop Booker at an I-40 truck stop northwest of the city.

"You've got a straight shot if you want to continue west," he told Booker. "Movers on this route know Alley Cat, so tell the drivers you worked with me." He then paid his lumper off with $100.

"That's too much," Booker said.

"Who's the boss here?" Cliff said, failing to put

any gruffness into his tone. "I say you are worth every nickel. This has been the best moving day I've had in years. I do believe you converted two white bureaucrats into human beings. You sure know how to close the distance between folks. I wish you were going in my direction, because I'd like to spend some more time with you. I don't think I've ever said that to a lumper, black or white."

"I'll be looking for you," Booker said. "Thanks for the extra."

Cliff pulled out and headed east toward a truck depot where he might schedule a return load to Virginia or Maryland. Booker took a bunk in the truck stop, showered, and decided to nap before he ate supper. He didn't wake up until after ten that night. It didn't matter what time he ate. The truck stop and its restaurant were a twenty-four-hour-a-day operation.

The late May night was mild and clear. Out of the glare of the light around the gas pumps, the moon and stars were clearly visible. Lines of trucks extended into the dark recesses of the parking area, their diesel engines purring as most of their drivers slept hidden away in their cab sleepers. Traffic was very light, a few trucks an hour stopping for coffee breaks. A dozen drivers occupied tables in the restaurant, chatting up the night waitresses or visiting with their buddies.

Booker ate his supper alone, and then, not ready to go back to bed, he decided to take in the night air with a walk around the truck stop. After one turn around the lot, a woman approached him behind the main building as he came in from the truck park.

On sight, the woman appeared to be in her mid to late thirties. She had bouffant blond hair that might have been a wig and not unattractive facial features accented with the kind of eye, lip, and cheek make-up a woman might wear to a party. Her skirt was so short that the light nylon Dallas Cowboys jacket she wore concealed everything but her shapely legs and high heels.

"Hello there, stranger," she began. "You're new. You staying overnight?"

"Yes, I am," Booker replied.

"Would you like to have some company?"

"That would be nice," Booker admitted.

The woman released her folded arms and allowed the unzipped front of the jacket to fall open. Her ample breasts were displayed in a skimpy halter top that exposed her cleavage and her midriff. She was justifiably proud of her figure.

"I've got my van parked in a nice, quiet corner of the lot so we won't be disturbed. What are you in the mood for?"

"We could talk or have some coffee," Booker said weakly, trying not to stare at her breasts.

"Maybe after," she said. "It's a slow night. None of my regulars have shown up. Have you got some cash?"

"Oh, sure. I had a big payday today," Booker confessed.

"Great. You want to go around the world?"

Booker was in an internal panic. A part of him

knew exactly what she was suggesting, and his body
was all in favor of it. He was having difficulty keeping those images out of his mind. The disciplined
silence that he had enjoyed for days and had begun
to take for granted was shattered in conflicting emotions. He knew temptation, and it was powerful. It
hit him where men are most vulnerable—their sexual
desire. He had almost forgotten. He had not even
masturbated since he left Norfolk. Had the woman
been toothless and obese, it would have been easier.
But this woman, breasts bulging and shapely legs
flexing, was a walking red-lipped fantasy. And he
had the cash to make it a reality.

Booker forced himself to reply, "I don't think so."

"OK. We could do a quickie for fifty. What about
that?" she asked.

"Are you sure that you don't want me to buy
you a supper?" Booker asked to procrastinate.

"Look, I'm not the girl next door, you simple old
fart. I'm a whore."

"Is that so?" Booker heard himself say.

"I do it for money, Honey. And it's worth every
damn cent."

"Is that so?"

"Well, just ask my customers. Mary Lou is the
class piece of ass on I-40. Everybody knows that."

"Is that so?"

"You are damn lucky I am available tonight. I
don't go down for just anybody. You have got to
be clean and look decent. I don't do niggers."

"Is that so?"

"Who told you different? It's a damn lie."

"Is that so?"

"You bet it is. I own a house. I've got kids in school. I'm no ordinary tramp, mister."

"Is that so?"

"Yes, that's so. I've got people who love me. People who respect me. I've got a lot more going for me than what you think."

"Is that so?"

"I don't have to do this. I've got a high school education. I went to beautician school and had a license."

"Is that so?"

"You bet it is. And I've got money in the bank, too. I drink a little bit, but I don't do drugs."

"Is that so?"

"I could open up a beauty salon if I wanted to. I'd be clean and legit."

"Is that so?"

"Why do you keep saying that?" she demanded.

"I don't know," Booker conceded. "Maybe I'm just trying to find out who you really are. Now that you've told me, I can't think of you as a whore. You are a beautiful person with a family and a career ahead. I'm glad I met you."

"You are crazy as hell!"

"Is that so?"

Mary Lou's eyes opened wide, and she took a deep breath of indignation. Without another word, she walked away, her heels clicking rapidly on the concrete apron. Then Booker could see the small rocks fly as she stormed into the gravel truck park. Booker walked to the side of the main building and watched her as she paced back and forth in front of the line of trucks. A trucker coming out of a cab on the line approached her. There were words, and Mary Lou turned her back on the man and walked away.

As he passed Booker, he remarked, "Watch out for Mary Lou. She's got a mean on tonight."

Ten minutes or so later, a customized Ford Econoline van sped between the lines of trucks from deep within the truck park, made an abrupt turn, and exited the truck stop. The windows were opaque so Booker could not see the driver. He watched the van speed out of sight and felt the return of fullness to the right side of his chest. He welcomed it as an old friend. And then he went to bed and slept the dreamless sleep of saints.

CHAPTER NINE

If Booker were ever going to wash his clothes in the truck stop coin laundry room, he needed another pair of pants and a change of underwear. He had over $150 in his pocket, so he was able to buy a pair of jeans, a belt, a western-style long-sleeve shirt, and another set of socks, underwear, and tee shirt. One of the drivers who had observed him stashing his backpack in an unlocked locker in the drivers' quarters advised him to get a combination lock, so he got that. He also added a plastic bottle of isopropyl alcohol. It seemed like a good purchase for massaging his feet. Because it killed bacteria, it might keep him from getting athlete's foot. After a shower, Booker would also pour an ounce of alcohol into his palm, rub his hands together, and apply them quickly to his arm pits as a deodorant. His grandfather had used bay rum in much the same manner and had lived into his nineties.

Booker, dressed out in his new jeans and shirt, was taking his overalls and underwear out of the dryer when a strange man stepped into the door frame.

"You Booker Jones?" he asked with some authority.

"Yes," Booker answered, wide-eyed that anyone had found him.

"I'm Willie Peel. Alley Cat said you might be here. We passed each other in Nashville this morning. He says that you are a good lumper. You want to go to Tulsa? I got a container of household goods."

"Sure," Booker said.

"We'll go on in today, lay over, and deliver tomorrow morning."

"Fine," Booker agreed.

The ride to Tulsa was about five hours. Sweet Willie owned his Freightliner and liked to work around the port of Savannah, near his home. He had retired from the army as a motor pool sergeant. He asked briefly about Booker's work experience and then concentrated on the CB radio, making contacts with other truckers as they traversed the country on I-40.

I-40 is a long road beginning near Wilmington, North Carolina, on the Atlantic coast; then, turning west at Durham, it runs all the way to Barstow, California. The route is a sunbelt across a region of dramatic population growth. At the end of May, with children out of school, another relocation season begins. Families who plan to move will need van line reservations during the summer months. Drivers will be in demand. Lumpers will find all the work they can stand.

Tulsa is a detour off I-40. At a point in history, Tulsa was the oil capital of the world. Wildcat oil rigs dotted the landscape. At another time, its territory was designated as the home of the five civilized

tribes: Cherokee, Choctaw, Chickasaw, Creek, and
Seminole. Today, Tulsa is a place where you begin
to sense the difference between the American West
and the South.

The containerized cargo that the crane had put
on Willie's flatbed trailer in Savannah had been
sealed in Amsterdam, Holland, a North Sea port. The
customers, Beth and Donald Smithson, were coming
home to Tulsa to retire after a life of following oil
rigs all over the world. Don's last assignment as a
project maintenance engineer was to shepherd a
floating oil rig platform from its construction site in
New Orleans across the ocean to Amsterdam. Contract disputes and oil prices held the rig in the
Dutch port for over a year before it could be
moved to its North Sea site and put into operation.
Don and a skeleton crew servicing the silent rig
had their easiest year of employment. Beth and Don
saw a lot of Europe that year and then set up
housekeeping in Amsterdam until the end of his
contract.

Booker was amazed at what you could learn if
you gave people a chance to talk. Don had an engineering degree, but he was informal and unpol-
ished from pushing men to do hazardous, tough jobs
all his working life. He dressed like a western ranch
foreman and had the weathered skin of a man who
works outdoors. Beth was the kind of woman you
get when you take a spunky ranch gal and tramp
her around the world for twenty or thirty years:
deep character, look-you-in-the-eye self-confidence,
and a gracious sense of humor.

Winn had never encountered such an adventure-some pair. Booker found them and the collection of artifacts from the Middle East, Asia, and Europe to be fascinating. It was another satisfying day on the job.

Don produced cold beers, and Willie and Booker toasted the Smithsons' retirement about four in the afternoon. Then the driver pointed the Freightliner back to I-40. Willie stopped to eat at the first siz-able truck stop near Sallisaw. He was going the op-posite way from Booker.

"Try to make it across Oklahoma, at least to Am-arillo, on your next jump," Willie advised. "When you hit the plains, water holes are few and far between. You might have to go on some jobs way off the superslab, but most drivers got to come back to it sooner or later."

He paid Booker $65 for the job.

"Did Don slip you anything extra?" Willie asked.

"He slipped me ten," Booker said.

"Good. They were good people."

After the meal together, before Willie had to go, Booker asked him for a favor.

"There are some people I need to contact, to tell them that I am OK. Will you send a telegram for me when you get back to Savannah?"

"Why don't you just call them?" Willie asked and then regretted that he had.

"It would be awkward," Booker explained.

"I understand," Willie said with empathy. "Sure, I'll do it."

Booker wrote the name, address, and message on

a blank sheet from Willie's trip logbook. It was addressed to Ellen Conover at a Norfolk, Virginia, address. The message read:

Don't worry. Am well. Need time to know myself.

Sorry to upset you. Love. Winn.

Booker offered Willie twenty dollars to cover the Western Union expenses. Sweet Willie would accept only ten.

"I might not get to send this until Friday," Willie advised.

"That's fine."

"But you can depend on me to send it."

"I know."

"And then I will forget everything about it," Willie assured him. "Personal is personal."

"Thanks."

"Do you mind me telling Alley Cat that we worked together? He'd get a kick out of that. He calls you Uncle Booker. I see why."

"Tell him."

"It may be weeks before we cross trails, but I get up into his neck of the woods fairly often. Sometimes we shoot the shit over coffee on I-95 in Virginia."

Booker waved Willie out of the truck stop and then went back in to reserve himself a bed, a shower, and a locker. By now it was routine. Some driver facilities were newer or cleaner than others but with familiarity they seemed to Booker like returning to the same barracks night after night. It was similar to his brief army experience. After a while, you begin to think of your barracks as your home. After one week on the road as a lumper, Booker saw the truck stop as his home. No matter where he was in the country, the truck stops were a constant. They looked the same. They felt and smelled the same. Even the food in the restaurants tasted the same. And until he knew them as individuals, all the characters around the truck stop appeared from the same casting office and costume department. They seemed habitual extras on the same movable stage.

That Friday, as promised, Willie sent the telegram from a Western Union office in Savannah and then threw away Booker's handwritten message. In keyboarding the message, only one mistake was made by the clerk. The second "n" in "Winn" was deleted.

In Norfolk, Ellen Conover was beset with messages. When Winston's disappearance had been reported in the second section of the Norfolk *Virginian-Pilot and Ledger-Star*, friends, associates, and strangers had begun to call and write with their sympathy and suggestions. The audience widened as regional newspapers picked the story off the Associated Press wire and used it as news filler.

Even from the beginning, there were hurtful notes and calls, cruel in their accusations of why Ellen had driven her husband away. Then the exposure expanded further as listings concerning the disappearance began to appear in national missing persons registries. Troubled people find twisted significance in certain newspaper articles and data banks. A number of them taunt the subjects of personal tragedies for their own mad purposes. Ellen

Conover had already been shocked and hurt by such communications.

When the telegram arrived, she excitedly took it to the police, who could not trace it beyond the Western Union office in Savannah. On further examination, the missing "n" in the sender name was noted. If Winn had actually sent the message, would he have spelled his own name wrong? Ellen concluded that the message was a cruel hoax, not unlike some of the crank letters and telephone calls she was receiving. The police agreed. The telegram was just another false lead.

CHAPTER TEN

Booker approached six drivers on Thursday morning. One of them was deadheading an empty trailer, and two others were going east. He got an offer to take a load to Fort Riley, Kansas, but turned it down as being too isolated. I-70 in Kansas eventually ran to Denver, but there would be few jobs along the way. Another driver would take him to Lubbock, Texas, but Booker heeded Sweet Willie's advice not to get marooned in the desert plains. The best offer seemed to be Santa Fe. The driver planned to go another eight hours, stop overnight en route, and then drive another four hours to get to his destination by noon on Friday.

Booker had no expectations about Santa Fe since Winn had never been there. He liked the idea, however, of a day off to rest his muscles. He had worked hard five of the eight days since leaving Norfolk. He realized that he had to pace himself until he lost weight and developed more strength. His weight had already fallen eleven pounds. It was starting to show in his face, although he hardly noticed it through the week's growth of beard.

The trip and overnight were routine. The driver, Bill Elder, was "Cowboy" on the CB radio. There were probably a hundred CB Cowboys on the road, but Bill was from Dallas, Texas, and had hauled steers before he became a Mayflower Van Lines driver, so he felt he had first rights to the handle. This Cowboy had been a trucker since his mid twenties and had been on the road for seventeen years. Bill was into his second marriage. His only daughter was graduating high school the following week and was already accepted to Abilene Christian University. Bill was into Christian gospel and pop music and had an impressive collection of cassette tapes that he constantly played under the noise of the CB radio.

About the third hour on the road, Bill brought himself to ask the critical question.

"Booker, are you saved?"

Booker did not pause. If he had, Bill would have questioned his doubts and maybe even pulled off the road to quote scripture from a stock of religious pamphlets that he carried amid the clutter on his dashboard. Some of Bill's proudest moments included getting a sinner down on his knees at the side of the highway and refusing to drive further until the man got saved.

"Yes," Booker testified. "I love the Lord with all my heart and try to do His will daily."

"Hallelujah," Bill erupted. "Praise God. It is so good to have a brother in Jesus on the job."

"Thank you," Booker said simply.

"What's your church?"

Booker subconsciously realized that the question was loaded with potential separation.

"My church right now is the fellowship of the highway. It is a kind of mission." Booker was being truthful in a language Bill might understand.

"Praise God," Bill said again. "My ministry is on the highway, too."

"Wherever two are gathered," Booker quoted.

"Praise God, and that's the truth."

The business of driving, especially when a driver is at peace with his companion, occupied most of the trip. When they stopped for the night, they ate together, and Bill said a long grace over their food. He gave Booker a few religious tracts with the suggestion that he leave some on the beds in the dormitory and at least one in the laundry room and locker room. Booker agreed.

"You never know when a lost soul might need it," Bill advised. "See you in the morning."

Arriving in Santa Fe was a marvel to Booker. The architecture, a blend of Pueblo adobe and Spanish colonial styles, was striking even from the highway. The morning sun bathing the layers of tan adobe houses on the hillsides was a brilliant light he had never seen before. The landscape was Spartan, unmarred by high-rise structures, unmodern in a lovely way. So many cities in America looked alike. If one were transported with a blindfold and deposited on an urban street, sight could not identify the place. Santa Fe was remarkably different.

The load was consigned to a retired military couple, an air force general, Anderson Little, and his wife. The home was off Canyon Road in the artist district of the community and was in the traditional adobe style, although it was quite new.

Marge Little was an accomplished water colorist, and Santa Fe was her retirement dream. She envisioned practicing her art to the extent of seeing her works displayed in one of the better galleries on San Francisco Street. Andy Little had substantial contacts in the military-industrial complex and was assured a few years of consulting work in the convenient California aviation industry. He also looked forward to playing a lot of golf.

The move-in required more time than it should have because Marge Little fussed over the placement of every piece of furniture. Both she and Andy were long used to a house staff of enlisted people and squadrons of junior officers who lived to please them. The general was not about to lift furniture or to bring in even a box of his own books. For the most part, he left the details to his wife and disappeared for the afternoon. Marge Little did not make excuses for him. She had moved into quarters by herself many times before.

Bill Elder kept quiet and cooperated with Mrs. Little, who offered no first name, although it was obvious to Booker that he was stressed by her attitude and behavior. When she finally released them, she had provided no food or drink and no gratuity.

"Big shots," Bill complained as they pulled away. "They are all alike. If there wasn't water in the faucets, we could have dehydrated for all they care.

Then, Madame General jerks us around for an extra hour without a tip. Who does she think she is?"

"She probably doesn't know," Booker responded.

"It's hard to pray for somebody like that," Bill said in exasperation.

"I guess that's our lesson," the lumper said.

Bill came to a stoplight and took the opportunity to look at Booker.

"Maybe it is. I noticed that you didn't say ten words all day."

"What was there to say?"

"Ha!" Bill exclaimed. "What was there to say? Exactly."

Bill wanted to start back to Texas right away so that he could be home on Saturday to see his daughter in her prom dress. Booker decided to stay in Santa Fe rather than being dropped back on the interstate, so Bill paid him $70 for the job and let him off across the Santa Fe River within walking distance of the center city plaza.

"God be with you," Bill said in parting.

"And with you," Booker replied.

The priority, as far as Booker's body was concerned, was food. He found the Plaza, flanked by the historic Palace of the Governors, expensive shops, and ornate Victorian buildings, but it was not the place for a poor man to eat. Booker wondered where the Indians ate who sat against El Palacio Real wall displaying their silver and turquoise jewelry on native blankets.

Down the block, he approached the first person he met who was not carrying a camera.

"Excuse me, could you recommend an inexpensive restaurant that serves traditional local dishes?"

The man looked surprised at the articulate stranger in overalls, checked his watch, and then gave directions to a working class restaurant favored by people who worked downtown.

Josie's Casa De Comida was in a converted house just outside the normal tourist track. It had a wide front porch and a large chalkboard where lunchtime patrons could post their claims to a table. Booker arrived very near closing. The place was so empty that he had to walk to the rear of the house and attract attention from voices in the kitchen. A dark-complexioned woman with Native American features showed him to a table and offered a menu.

"What do you suggest? I'm new to your area, but I would very much like to sample your food."

"Are you very hungry?" she asked.

"Yes, I am."

"Let me fix you one of the combination plates."

"Fine. Whatever you recommend."

"Do you want red or green chile?"

"I don't know," Booker admitted.

"I'll bring both on the side," she smiled. "You might find it too hot if you are not used to it."

When the entree plate arrived, it was huge. A side plate was also provided with sopaipillas, a fried bread. Then the waitress refilled his water glass and put the small bowls of red and green chile on the table. Booker was aware that three older women had come out of the kitchen to watch him. They greeted him when they were noticed. The waitress explained.

"They are waiting for you to taste the chile."

The plate contained pinto beans served whole, not refried; blue cornmeal tortillas filled with meat and cheese; posole, a type of hominy cooked with chile and pork; chile rellenos, green chilies stuffed with cheese, batter-dipped and fried; and finally a pair of chicken enchiladas.

"Where do I start?" Booker appealed.

"Try one of the chiles on your tortillas or enchiladas," the waitress encouraged.

Booker applied the green chile sauce on an enchilada and bit into it.

"Wow!" he said after he had swallowed.

The women laughed.

"Do you like it?" one of them asked.

"Yes. I think I do. I'll just have to get used to it."

"The green is hotter than the red today," another woman advised.

"Thank you," Booker acknowledged as he reached for the water.

For the next thirty minutes, Booker worked on the entrees with careful application of the chiles. Whenever one of the women came to the door of the kitchen, he would gesture at the food and say, "Wonderful! Wonderful!"

Early into the meal, Booker was aware that he was sweating. His hair was wet, and sweat began to be evident under his arms and in the hollow of his chest. By mid meal, he was soaking wet. Drops formed on the tip of his nose and fell off his ear lobes. He drank glass after glass of water but kept on eating. Truly, the food was delicious and different. He thought he would get over its being hot.

The women hiding and peeking from the kitchen could stand it no longer. They emerged to surround Booker with laughter and care. One of them had a handful of extra napkins and carefully mopped his face. He laughed along with them and reached out to touch their hands.

"What do you think?" the waitress asked as she removed the plates.

"Best meal I ever had," Booker exclaimed with chile tears in his eyes.

The women exploded with laughter and each one of them had to kiss him on the cheek or forehead.

"Can I have the check, please?" The request only made them laugh more.

"Let me bring you a cool natillas before you go," one of the cooks offered.

"It's a vanilla milk pudding," another explained.

"Maybe I should pay first," Booker suggested.

"No. No. This is free for you. Everything free."

"Please, please," Booker protested.

"You eat your natillas," the senior woman said. "We'll get tea and join you."

During the next half hour, the women closed the restaurant and relaxed with Booker at his table. They asked questions, and he explained to them about being a lumper. They looked at his backpack and wondered with glances to each other why this well-spoken, well-mannered gentleman led such a life!

Booker took the opportunity of their friendship to ask about accommodations.

"Where can a working man find a place to stay in Santa Fe?" he asked. "I can't afford the tourist hotels."

The women looked at each other and then began to speak in a foreign language that Booker knew was not Spanish.

"It is decided," the oldest one announced. "You will stay with Maria's great-grandmother. She has a nice room. Can you pay ten dollars a night?"

"Yes, of course."

"Nita will also give you breakfast." She pronounced the name broadly as Nee-TAH, accenting the second syllable.

"That's very generous," Booker said. "Perhaps I can help her in some way."

"I'm Maria," the woman who had been his waitress said. "Perhaps you could chop some firewood and bring water."

"Yes, I would be glad to. Shouldn't we call her to make sure it will be OK?"

"Nita has no telephone and no inside water. She lives in a pueblo. Do you mind?" Maria asked.

"No. I will be honored to share her pueblo."

"Nita is old. She does not speak much English," the oldest woman advised.

"I'm sure we can get along," Booker said.

The women nodded their heads in agreement and spoke a few more words in the unknown language.

"I'll drive you to the pueblo if you are ready," Maria said.

CHAPTER ELEVEN

During the ten-mile ride to the pueblo, the sun began to set. They were traveling north of Santa Fe with the western sky ablaze. Hot white light behind the silhouetted houses and hills gave way to bright yellow, pink, and orange bands that then faded into a purple night. The sky seemed much larger than skies remembered in the East. Booker cleared his mind of comparisons and allowed himself to enjoy its nameless beauty.

"Our pueblo is very old," Maria explained. "One of the earliest to make contact with the Spanish. Few anglos have ever stayed overnight. But we think you will be good for Nita."

"Tell me about her," Booker said.

"Nita keeps the old ways. She is over ninety, but she still grinds corn on the metates and makes piki bread. She is the elder woman of our clan, The Deer People. She is the keeper of our tribal life secrets. She knows the ceremonies and the dances and the songs of women. Many times she has led the Animal Dancers down from the mountains in the snows of January. In bare feet, with her face painted with red disks, she had the place of honor for the Hunting Dance. For as long as I can remember, Nita has taught the Corn Dance in the kiva of the Summer People. No outsider can ever know these things."

"What is the kiva of the Summer People?" Booker asked.

"Every pueblo or village is built around a ceremonial plaza. If you live on the north side of the plaza, you are Winter People. On the south side, you are Summer People. A kiva is a meeting hall. A man belongs to the clan of his mother. The pueblo is made up of clans. Some members of the clan are Winter People. Some are Summer People."

"I understand. Nita must have a very large clan."

"The Deer People are many, but most do not choose the old ways. They have ancestor homes in their pueblo, but they come only for Feast Days, or they come to sell crafts to the visitors. Then they go home to their TVs and their washing machines."

"Where do you live?" Booker asked.

"With my TV and my washing machine," Maria laughed.

"But you respect the old ways," Booker said.

"Yes, the old ways are our religion. The Spanish built mission churches in our pueblos and forced us to carry Spanish names, but we are Anasazi. That is who we really are as a culture. Nita has preserved the culture and religion for us while we were foolish. Now we realize how precious and brave she is. She has already handed down her secrets, now she waits for death. We try to do things to keep her with us."

"Like me, for example?" Booker suggested with a smile.

"Nita will stay alive with a man to feed. She will think ten dollars a day is a fortune, but she will act offended that we brought you because you are not of our clan. We are teasing her back to life."

"I understand."

"Be kind to her. She is a great soul," Maria said softly.

"I will," Booker promised.

"For some reason, at Josie's, we felt we could trust you."

The pueblo was off a highway that left the few street lights and bumped along in the darkness of a dirt road. It was almost a surprise when the adobe buildings appeared in the car headlights. The village plaza was deserted, and there seemed to be no lights in the low lines of sand-colored structures. When Maria turned off the engine and the headlights, the profound silence and darkness surrounded them.

Maria produced a flashlight and instructed Booker to remain in the car until she made contact with Nita. Soon the bouncing cylinder of light was gone, and Booker had to wrestle with Winn's imagination as he waited in darkness.

When Maria reappeared, she apologized for the length of time she had been away. "I had to get your room ready," she advised. "There is a basin and a pitcher of water on the wash stand in your room. I'll show you the chemical toilet to use tonight. Don't leave the house until morning. Then you can use the outhouse." Maria was already leading him among the smooth adobe plastered walls. "Nita has gone to her room. She is up at dawn. There are only oil lamps and the fireplace for light, so she goes to bed early. You can meet her in the morning when she makes you breakfast."

"When do I pay her?" Booker asked.

"Do not give her money directly. I will show you a pot where you may put it. Since you are a guest, Nita would never ask you to pay."

The door to Nita's house had once been painted yellow, but the weather had worn the color out except in the corners of its recessed panels. When they opened the door, the only light in the room emanated from a small, oval hearth built into the adobe wall. The fire consisted of a few pieces of wood, cut by an ax into narrow strips. The room had a pleasant incense smell.

"What is the smell?" Booker asked.

"It's from the piñon wood in the fireplace," Maria said. "The fire burns slowly and the heat stays within the thick walls."

"It is very comfortable and dry," Booker observed.

"There are three rooms and a partially covered courtyard out back. This room is used for cooking, eating, sitting, working, everything. Nita sleeps in the closed room, and you sleep in the room with the door to the courtyard. Nita may have to pass by you to use the toilet just outside the courtyard door or to get food stuff stored out there. We hang the chile peppers on the shelter poles and keep pots of dried fruits and corn outside. Sleep late if you want to. Nita will not disturb you."

Booker's room was furnished with a low single bed on a rough-hewn wooden frame placed against a side wall, a washstand, and a set of shelves made from the same wood during the same bygone era. The oil lamp on the top of the shelving piece provided the only light.

A beautiful Indian blanket was turned down to reveal coarse-woven tan cotton sheets. The floor seemed to be a reddish tile. Pegs in the adobe walls were available for hanging garments.

"This is immaculate," Booker said in appreciation. "The floor is something I have never seen."

"It is a clay floor," Maria said.

"But it seems almost polished. And the rich color?"

"This is a floor made in the traditional way. It is adobe clay mixed with deer blood and then pounded until the compound is smooth. It becomes glossy like tile."

Booker put his backpack down on the clean floor. "This is wonderful," he said, extending his arms to the room.

"As good as the green chile?" Maria teased.

"Yes," Booker replied, matching her smile. "As good as the green chile."

"Then I will say goodnight. I hope you are comfortable. I know that you are not hungry."

Booker saw Maria out the front door and then retired to his room for a brief wash-up and then bed. As he blew out the lamp, he could not stop himself from remembering the faces of the people he had met over the past ten days since leaving

Norfolk: Bell, the street person who had given him a name; Steve, the saint who had blessed him; Slim Jim, who had confirmed him as a lumper; Janice, who taught him line dancing; Little John in the burley arms of Bad Bobby, a man who was less bad than desperate; Alley Cat and Paul and Zena, all so generous; and Mary Lou, the woman who saw herself as a whore. Did he encounter the four of them in a single day? And Sweet Willie and the Smithsons in Tulsa. Then Cowboy Bill Elder, another born-again man who saw himself as very different from General Little and his wife. And finally Maria and the women in the kitchen at Josie's. The richness of his abundant life flooded into his eyes, and he was more grateful to be alive than he had ever been before.

In the morning, light came into Booker's room from a rectangular window about the size of a telephone book, on the courtyard exterior wall. He dressed in his jeans and only shirt and went outside in search of the outhouse. It was a chilly morning, so he retrieved his jacket and then found the privy some thirty yards out in a field behind the adobe chain of houses. There were few such structures in sight, so Booker assumed this to be the outhouse Maria had mentioned. Winn had never experienced an outhouse.

The thin door, held to the narrow upright structure by leather hinges, was opened to reveal a single-holed bench suspended above an open pit. The smell was mildly offensive with chemical overtones. Booker suspected that the courtyard toilet, a molded plastic bowl and seat, was a concession to Nita's age. However, finding the outdoor privy in the middle of the night or in a deep snow would make anyone prefer the nearer john.

The door pulled closed with a leather thong which looped over a wooden peg. Booker relieved himself and stared at a point on the backside of the crude door that had been woven from branches. Although the privy itself was probably moved from time to time and a new hole dug, anyone seated on the toilet bench would have faced the same focus. Judging from the age of the privy, generations of Pueblo Indians must have struggled with their bowels and their dilemmas here as the wind made soft whistles through the cracks of the house. Before the Catholic priests taught them Christian modesty, the Indians probably went into their fields, dug a small cat hole with a stick, and did their business as fertilizer. Today, in preparation for Feast Days, the Pueblo government must have to rent a truckload of privy-sized port-a-johns to accommodate the crowds. Such were the speculations of Booker's mind until he recognized the process and ended it.

"Not quite the morning prayer of renewal and celebration, is it?" He laughed and then forgave himself.

A quick wash and tooth brushing and Booker went into the main room to seek Nita. He first saw her sitting on a low milking-size stool in front of a wood fire stove. The stove, like the fireplace, was built into the adobe wall and they shared a common chimney. A piece of heavy metal was the cooking surface. Three steaming bowls were being tended by Nita.

Booker stopped in the middle of the room so as not to alarm her and called to her in a low voice, pronouncing her name the way Maria had, Nee-TAH. When the old woman turned to see him, he bowed his head as a sign of respect and said, "Thank you for taking me into your home. My name is Booker."

Nita nodded to him in recognition and motioned to the table where a place was set with a shallow bowl, a cup, and a spoon. The ceramic pieces were of an Indian design and appeared antique.

The meal consisted of hot hominy made from dried white corn, which resembled Southern grits, topped by stewed fruit sweetened with honey. The beverage was a hot herbal tea. Booker enjoyed the new tastes, and he demonstrated his pleasure to Nita by sounds and gestures understood by all cultures who enjoy eating. Nita brought her cup of tea to the table to watch Booker eat. It was not until he had finished did the expression on her face change. Then she allowed herself a small smile that was not lost on her guest.

Booker remembered his offer to help with chopping firewood, so he mimicked a man using an ax, and Nita led him to the courtyard where the wood was kept. The piñon logs were neatly stacked, and Booker could see where they had been split and then cut into strips for the cookstove and fireplace. Nita showed him an ax, a hatchet, and a sharpening stone.

Whoever had sawed the piñon logs had provided them in a short uniform length. They were not so thick that they could not be split with an ax and then wedge cut with the hatchet into kindling-size strips. This seemed to be the size preferred, judging from the wood box near the fireplace. After the inside box was filled, Booker continued to work until all the logs were split and many of them were reduced to a neat stack of strips. He had no idea how long the effort took. He was enjoying the sunshine, the mountain air filled with the hint of piñon, and a quiet beyond traffic. The sounds were of birds, the occasional barking of pueblo dogs, and the solid crack of the ax or the splintering of wood by the hatchet. For him, it was a meditation, the labor focusing the mind so that the spirit could float free.

When he tired of the chopping task, he decided to empty and clean the chemical toilet. He needed water from the Summer People's spring. Nita pointed the way. Booker found a pipe extending three feet off the ground capped by a faucet. The mountain water was cold and sparkling clear. He cupped his hand and took mouthfuls of water to satisfy his thirst. The water had body and an effervescence he had not associated with water before. He could not help himself from saying aloud, "Now this is water!"

Nita provided a form of lye made from piñon ash to clean and recharge the toilet. Booker did not see her expression of disbelief as she witnessed the anglo cleaning her stool. His final chore was to make trips with a bucket to the spring faucet and refill the supply of cooking and drinking containers as well as the pitchers for the wash basins. Then he left Nita to her privacy and ventured out into the pueblo.

When the volunteer helpers from her clan arrived after the noon sun to perform the chores too difficult for Nita, they found all the work done, plus a week's worth of firewood. Nita told them that a white-bearded anglo man who was boarding with her had done all the chores before they arrived. They accepted tea from Nita and sat with her for an hour, but they did not believe the story about the anglo. What anglo would ever use a chamber pot, much less empty and clean one?

Cars and vans were parked at the head of the plaza, and Booker joined the fifteen to twenty tourists who were exploring the open doors of the pueblo. Access was usually limited to the front rooms of individual houses which had been converted to daytime shops. Three of the open rooms featured silver and turquoise jewelry made by artisans belonging to the pueblo. One room sold woven goods such as blankets and traditional dresses. Two rooms were devoted to pottery traded from distant pueblos. Booker saw unusual black-on-black matte-finished bowls, brown micaceous ware, and geometric black and white Acoma pots. Another shop sold books and miscellaneous Indian artifacts such as dolls and arrowheads. Booker's favorite shop sold ristras, the hanging strings of red chilies, blue corn and cornmeal, dried game meat, dried fruit, various types of beans, and fresh, outdoor-adobe-oven-baked bread.

The shops did not seem commercial. The display

of goods was homelike. Even the jewelry was simply laid out on a blanket-covered table. There were no cash registers, no background music, and no signage. Although you were greeted when you entered, the proprietor, usually an Indian woman, did not speak further unless she was spoken to first. In most shops, a small fire kept the chill from the open door off the room.

Booker made a meal from a loaf of Indian bread, a length of smoked venison jerky and the effervescent spring water.

The koshari, or pueblo police, was represented by a man Booker's age who wore no uniform and directed the visitors like a gentle tour guide. It reminded Booker that he had heard no Indian at the pueblo raise his voice. The policeman told Booker where he might walk along a path leading to the mountains, but cautioned him against entering the pueblo cemetery near the route.

"The pueblo is not only our traditional home, it is also our spiritual center. We ask visitors to respect our ceremonial places as they would their own churches."

Booker went far along the path until the sun began its majestic end-of-day show. He was able to enjoy the spectacle and still find Nita's door before nightfall. He considered it the end of a perfect day.

The next time Booker saw Nita, she was dressed in a traditional long hand-woven dark blue wool dress draped over the right shoulder and under the left arm and held in place with a silver brooch. Her white hair was combed straight to her shoulders, framing a wrinkled face that seemed, with its large nose and chiseled cheek bones, like a deep copper relief. She wore beautiful jewelry consisting of a substantial silver and turquoise necklace, companion bracelets on both wrists, and several rings on each hand. Soft leather shoes and an intricately woven light blanket worn like a shawl completed her outfit. Maria and one of the other women from Josie's were already in attendance.

Booker, who had seen Nita only in a simple, un-adorned house dress, paid his first respects to her.

"Nita," he said in the Indian way, "you look like a queen."

No one translated the remarks, but they did have the effect of making Nita raise her head in a regal pose.

"Is today a Feast Day?" Booker asked of Maria, noting that all the women were wearing their jewelry.

"No," Maria said with a smile. "Today is Sunday. We are going to church. Come, we are serving breakfast. You remember Pearl from Josie's, don't you?"

"Yes. Pearl, good to see you again."

Pearl served the same meal Booker had eaten the previous morning.

"Would it be possible for me to join you for church? I only have these jeans and shirt."

The women made brief comments to each other in their strange language, and then Maria spoke for them.

"You will sit with us," she said. "Are you Catholic?"

"No," Booker admitted, "but I am reverent."

The word required translation, but the women seemed satisfied.

The mission church at the pueblo had not been a part of its original design. It was set off at the far end of the plaza on the Winter People's side of the village. The interior of the mission was as spare as its adobe exterior. The heavy beam altar table was raised and centered on a painted wooden relief of the crucified Christ. On each side were crudely carved and painted statues of saints and stands of lit candles. Four rows of benches flanked the center aisle. The remainder of the worshipers were expected to stand on the clay floor behind them. On this Sunday, a congregation consisting mainly of old women and their female relations was not enough to fill the benches.

The priest was perhaps too young to relate to these seniors in his parish. He did not speak their native language, and he did not have time to socialize since this mass was the second of four that he was scheduled to perform at separate pueblos prior to one o'clock. Nevertheless, Booker appreciated the mass as a gathering of very reverent people who brought to the place a sense of peace and devotion. It was very easy for him to depose his mind in this environment and rest in the spiritual heart.

Maria and Pearl sat on either side of Nita with Booker nearest Pearl on the center aisle. The mass was in English. After the service, with the young priest off to his next stop, Booker asked Maria how Nita understood the sermon.

Maria seemed amused. "Nita speaks four languages. Two of the five Pueblo tongues, Spanish, and English."

"You said Nita didn't speak much English," Booker said as a mild protest.

"Right. She does not often speak English. But she understands almost everything."

"Am I welcome to stay a few more days?" Booker asked.

"Yes," Maria replied, "if you don't talk too much. Nita prefers to talk in her own language."

Booker nodded agreement.

"You are also invited to join us for Sunday dinner. One of Nita's granddaughters—my aunt—is having us. Everyone wants to meet the anglo who cleans Nita's chamber pot."

The dinner was held in a modest house outside of Santa Fe. Although there were chickens free in the yard, the outbuildings, trucks, and stacks of wood along the dirt driveway made it seem that the occupants were in the firewood business. Nita's granddaughter, a portly Indian woman over fifty, set out a generous buffet for her husband, her son and daughter-in-law, the three clan relatives, and Booker. Most of the family conversation was in Spanish. Although the two men were reserved, maybe even suspicious of Booker, they treated him in a very polite manner. The hostess led Booker to the table to be served first and helped him identify each dish. There were two baked chickens with the soft meat already pulled off the bones, accompanied by a natural gravy flavored with baked chilies. On the side were pinto beans, white rice, corn on the cob, squash, and a stack of fresh tortillas. After dinner, sopa, a type of bread pudding, and a hot tea would be served.

Booker was surprised that he was not asked a lot of qualifying questions about his origins and his purpose for being in Santa Fe. The women grouped together in the dining room, while the men found places in the living room. Booker was invited to sit on a sofa and put his plate on a coffee table. The furnishings were working class, but definably Southwestern. Deer and antelope antlers were mounted on one wall. The sofa was draped with an Indian blanket. Another blanket, probably an antique, hung on the wall. An ornate gun rack with two shotguns and a high-powered rifle stood in one corner.

Well into the meal, Ernest Silva, the host, attempted to make conversation with Booker.

"Maria says that you move furniture."

"Yes," Booker replied.

Some minutes went by as the men continued to eat before Ernest spoke again.

"Do you seek work in Santa Fe?"

"Yes. I have traveled far, and now I wish to stop in one place for a while," Booker explained.

"That is good," Ernest agreed.

More time elapsed, and then Booker said, "I see your wood and your trucks. It looks like a good business."

Ernest's son, Carlos, looked to his father as if seeking his permission to speak and then answered.

"We cut mesquite and piñon for the restaurants," Carlos said.

"I like very much the smell of piñon burning in the fireplace," Booker said.

"Mesquite is very good to cook meat and chicken and fish," Ernest commented.

The men finished their plates and were offered seconds. Booker followed their example and took more of the delicious chicken with its pungent chile gravy over the rice. When the men were settled again in the living room, Ernest asked, "Would you like to help us with the wood?"

Without hesitation, Booker answered, "Yes, I would."

Minutes passed as the men concentrated on their food. Then Carlos said, "This is our busy season. The tourists are coming. Many restaurants want our wood."

Another long pause ended when Ernest asked, "Can you work tomorrow?"

"Yes," Booker answered, "but I have no watch and no transportation."

The two Indians smiled at each other.

"Be on the highway outside the pueblo when the sun rises," Ernest said. "We will come for you."

When Booker was gone, Carlos made a wager with his father that the anglo would not be on the highway at sunrise.

"He did not even ask the wage," Carlos argued. "Suppose he discovers that mesquite trees have thorns."

"This is the anglo who cleans Nita's chamber pot," Ernest rebutted. "He will do anything."

"He will do women's work," Carlos observed. "But will he do the work of men?"

"We will see," his father said.

Returned to the pueblo, Nita went to her room where Maria and Pearl helped her undress. Booker made a fire in the fireplace to warm up the house, and then he went about the chamber pot and water carrying chores. He said goodbye to the two women outside on a return trip carrying a pail of water. He was surprised when each of them gave him a warm hug before departing.

When he entered the house, Nita was sitting in a chair in front of the fire. She was back in her house dress, her jewelry put away. Her festive Sunday blanket was replaced by an old blanket that had lost most of its color. Booker filled the last pot with water and then took one of the table chairs and joined Nita at the fire.

They sat in silence as the fire flickered and crackled. The design of the fireplace flue demanded little from the fuel. Booker infrequently added a stick at a time to keep the fire going. The large dinner meal was working its content, and Booker, knowing that he need not make conversation with Nita, relaxed completely. He lost the track of time as he was practiced to do. Perhaps an hour had passed because there was the dull glow of twilight at the window when he opened his eyes. Nita was softly singing in her native tongue, easily rocking back and forth in her chair in time to the music of her voice.

Although Booker could not understand the lyrics, and the music was totally alien to him, he knew that Nita was making a prayer. Its form was reminiscent of a chant, but Booker did not want to analyze or appreciate it as form. He wanted to go into it and ride its tonality. And so he began to rock gently in time with Nita. When next his mind came into focus, the fire was reduced to embers and the window totally dark.

Nita left her chair and began to make tea. Booker added wood to the fire and lit the two oil lamps in the room. They ate a supper of cold tortillas wrapped around leftovers from the Silvas' chickens. They did not require much.

Before they retired to their rooms, Booker shared with Nita his concern about waking up before sunrise. Her only response was to take his right hand into hers and to pat his hand with reassurance. He gave her a smile that said, "I will not worry."

CHAPTER TWELVE

He was awake, and he did not know if he had awakened by his own biological clock or because Nita was standing near his bed. As he stirred, she left the room.

It was still dark outside and chilly at their altitude of 7,000 feet, but the stove fire warmed the main room. Booker's breakfast of Indian tacos made with puffy frybread and hot tea was on the table. After he ate, he sat in silence as Nita sang a chant-like song which he took to be a kind of blessing.

With the song ended, Nita opened the door for her guest, and he went out and began the more than half mile walk to the highway. When he reached the single street light on the main road, the first rays of dawn appeared over the mountains. A few minutes later, Ernest Silva's truck stopped to pick him up. Booker could not help from wondering how Nita had timed the morning without a clock.

In the truck cab with Ernest and Carlos, the father spoke first. "I see you have your work gloves."

"Yes," Booker said, displaying the gloves he had used to move furniture.

"He has gloves, Carlos," the father said, reminding his son.

"Yes, I see," Carlos said with some resignation.

"I believe," Ernest said to Booker, "that Carlos is going to buy us a big lunch today. Is that not right, Carlos?"

The morning job was miles off any highway Booker recognized, down dusty dirt roads, and then off the road onto a scrub plain. The truck stopped beside piles of thorny trees which seemingly had been cut, gathered, and left to dry.

"This is mesquite," Ernest said with a gesture that included the plain. "It will grow in poor soil even in a drought. See the yellow flowers? Bees love mesquite."

"Be glad we don't cut trees in summer," Carlos added. "Too many bees."

The work consisted of cutting the mesquite branches into a standard length, stripping off the bark, and then tying the wood into bundles. The tools were on the truck, and although there was some technique to avoiding the thorns, the labor was simple, if intensive. Booker learned the process quickly and then attempted to get into the rhythm of work established by the father and son.

The sun was partially obscured by overcast, but the day warmed to a comfortable working temperature. As they worked, the two Indians began to softly sing a tribal song. At a pause, Booker asked, "Is that a work song?"

"It is the gathering wood song," Ernest said. "We have a song for doing all our chores. For drawing water. For walking the trail of a hunt. For picking corn. For grinding corn. Almost everything."

The men worked for five hours on a thermos of coffee. The bed of the open eighteen-foot truck was half filled with mesquite three bundles high.

"We make deliveries now," Ernest said as he collected the tools. "And Carlos will buy us a big lunch with cold beer."

The delivery route stopped at the service doors of three upscale restaurants advertising mesquite grilling as its specialty. Ernest went in to do the business and Carlos and Booker unloaded the required bundles of wood.

It was half past one when they finally stopped for lunch at a country restaurant catering to Spanish-speaking locals. Ernest encouraged Booker to order anything from the menu, even a beefsteak, but Booker stayed with the daily special of beans, rice, and enchiladas. Even the stoic Carlos seemed relieved, and he joined his father in a second beer. Booker politely declined the beer and drank iced tea.

The wages for the day were $25, and Booker was back at the pueblo before four in the afternoon. For the remainder of the week, the routine was the same except that some days they used chainsaws to reduce previously cut scrub pine trees into logs and then a gasoline-powered log splitter to further render the logs into cords of piñon firewood.

On Tuesday afternoon, Booker returned to his room to find his jeans, shirt, socks, and underwear clean and folded on his bed. On Wednesday, the dirty overalls he had been wearing and his other set of underclothes had been cleaned. He expressed his gratitude to Nita, but he was not sure that she had done the washing.

On Thursday, he brought Nita a bag of hard candies and a large sirloin steak that he had purchased at a convenient grocery store when the Silvas' truck stopped for gas.

Although nothing had been discussed, Nita was now furnishing Booker his suppers. On Tuesday, she had a large quantity of hot water waiting for him when he arrived from work. He got the message and took a standing bath in the roofed section of the rear courtyard before he put on his cleaned clothes.

On Friday the work day ran into sunset, and Ernest seemed in no hurry to return Booker to the pueblo.

"An important man would like to see you tonight," Ernest said as they left the highway for the dirt road to the plaza.

"Fine," Booker said.

"I will take you to him now."

Booker was fatigued from work and looking forward to Nita's supper, but he made no objection.

The door to the man's house was on the second level of the Winter People. Booker followed Ernest up a tall ladder made of poles with steps tied into place by leather thongs. They crossed the roof and entered a dimly firelit room. Ernest showed Booker to a bench at a table near the center of the room and then wordlessly withdrew and closed the door behind him.

Booker became aware that there was another person in the room seated across from his position in the shadow of a wall. He quelled his impulse to speak and began to practice the discipline of waiting without speculation. He took deep breaths and let the air out slowly to calm his respiration and heart rate. There was a comforting stillness in the room that warranted no defense. Booker closed his eyes and relaxed into the silence. A period of half an hour passed before the Pueblo man spoke.

"Nita's clan has told me that you have a noble spirit. I feel it is so. I give you the welcome our pueblo gives to a friend."

"Nita and her family have been very generous to me. I am grateful to be their friend," Booker replied.

"How is it possible for you to pray with Nita and be at peace?" the man asked as he moved his chair into the light closer to Booker.

"It is a thing I have learned in the emptiness of my mind," Booker answered.

"And how did you quiet the mind? Did you sing sacred songs or perform rituals?"

"No," Booker explained. "I was reborn."

"Oh," the Indian said in reflection. "What were you before your rebirth? Do you remember?"

"Yes, I was a business man who sold land."

The Indian man was quiet for a long minute and then asked, "And you have quit selling land to practice peace?"

"Yes," Booker answered.

"This is an important sign," the man said. "The anglo must learn that the land does not belong to him to buy and sell. It is he who belongs to the land."

"It is true," Booker affirmed.

"Would you like for me to tell you how we came to this land?"

Booker pulled his bench closer to the older man and nodded.

"In the beginning, we were Anasazi. We lived with the land in peace. Then raiders came from tribes in the north to attack us, steal our goods, and carry us off as slaves. A great drought came as a sign that we must move south. And so we came to build our pueblos where the soil was rich and the water abundant along the river valley known now as Rio Grande."

"Then the Spanish came to exchange our gold for their religion. They oppressed us, and we made a war on them and drove them away. But they came back to Santa Fe and made a bloody victory over our pueblos. They stole our Indian names and forced us to take their names, their language, and their religion, or they would kill us. But we kept our names and our ancient rules in secret."

"The Spanish built a highway to Mexico City. They called it Camino Real. Then, from the east, the anglos made the Santa Fe Trail. People came to trade and to mine and to hunt, and we became unwanted in our own land. Then the Americans made a war on Mexico, and, like cattle, we then belonged to them."

"The anglos cut the mountain forests bare so that the rains came down in floods and destroyed our planted fields. They brought diseases our medicine men did not know how to cure, and so we died in great numbers.

"Today we play the part assigned to us. We make our baskets, our pottery, and our jewelry, and dance our sacred dances for the tourists. We are put on display as a dead culture and a dying people. But I say to you that they do not know us. We were here in harmony with the land before them, and we will remain here when they are gone. They do not have souls to keep their treaty with God. We know His Spirit, and we obey."

"That is my purpose," Booker said, "to know and obey His Spirit."

"We believe that is true. That is why you were brought to me. I feel your soul in the silence, and there is no ripple, only submission. In our secret life, Nita is the Chief Old Woman. I am the cacique, the chief of our religion. Our Pueblo governor does our business, but my position is not known to outsiders. You may call me Joseph."

"Thank you, Joseph, for your trust."

"Would you like to sweat with us?" Joseph asked.

"Yes. What does it mean to sweat?"

"We make a fire in a kiva house without doors or windows. When the stones in the pit are very hot, we climb down through a hatch in the roof. I sing the ancient prayers, and we sweat together as a way of purification. Only serious believers can enter the sweat lodge. We prepare ourselves to listen for the voice of The Great Spirit. Often He speaks to us in visions."

"You honor me," Booker acknowledged. "I will prepare myself to listen."

"You are wise. We all must fast and pray before entering the sweat lodge. No man can bring his trouble into that place, or God will not speak."

"I understand," Booker said with clarity.

"This will be done on Sunday while the women go to church. We will sweat for many hours. And when it is done, we will wash ourselves and then eat. Nita will make us piki bread. Her piki stone is a great treasure. Nita honors you with her piki bread."

CHAPTER THIRTEEN

The simplicity of pueblo life helped Booker to see how technical advances had separated humankind from its spiritual Self. As people rushed to progress, they left behind their instincts for honoring creation. Modern society viewed the traditional Native American lifestyle and religion as primitive. And yet the quantum mechanics of today's physics had discovered that energy is not infinitely divisible. The heart of the matter cannot be quantified. It is pure. It is infinite. It appears interconnected to everything. So when the Native Americans and all other so-called primitive peoples recognized the spirit within rocks and trees and animals as well as man, they were closer to Reality than the arrogant societies who judged them.

Maria had said that her people had been foolish to abandon the traditions that Nita had preserved for them. The consequences of emulating the anglos were alcoholism and spiritual poverty. The home, the primary focus of life where every family head was a priest, was destroyed. In its place were objects of desire and the idea that these objects were the prerequisites of happiness. These objects were false gods.

The Ancient Ones had prayed for rain and for a good hunting season. Give us this day our daily bread. And in the grinding of corn on the metates stones or in the slaughtering of a white-tail deer, they sang prayers of thanksgiving to the spirit of the corn and the spirit of the deer. Can any church litany or Mozart Requiem do more to honor the Creator? Can the mind, as a repository of experience, discipline itself to a nobler expression?

Booker thought not. For him, the pueblo was a sanctuary. It was both a refuge and a place of worship. He was not separate from these Indian people. He was part of their collective spirit. The joining required no knowledge of their beliefs or their rituals. He joined them in the silence of their minds where the spiritual heart was revealed. The kinship could not be articulated. No words in any language had approximated it. Religions that could not teach it referred to it as a mystery and required their congregations to have faith in its potential. Few Western individuals since the Renaissance had experienced the quiet mind and the resulting revelation of interconnection, yet it was a common reality to primitive tribes isolated from the madness of the modern world.

And the few primitive peoples remaining knew that their common Earth Mother was sick. They witnessed the water and the trees disappearing, and they called out, "Little Brother, stop killing our Mother. Put aside your greed and listen to Her."

Winn Conover concluded from what he saw on television that the planet Earth was doomed and

that the ongoing destruction was being offered as
entertainment: a last Roman orgy of excess before
the final fall. The realization had driven him inward
to search for solutions.

Booker Jones, able to achieve a quiet mind for
extended periods, was exempt from the Apocalypse.
There was no need for the ultimate destruction of
evil for the good to triumph. Evil was a thought,
like other silly, insane thoughts dominating the
mind. The thoughts themselves separated Booker
from what was good and true. Thoughtlessness was
the prayer without ceasing. In the absence of
thought was God. This was what the ancients had
learned. This was the secret of life and relationship.
It was available to every person regardless of education, power, or wealth. If it were not so, God
would be a cruel potentate made in the image of
Man. These were not philosophical ideas in the
mind of Booker Jones. This was a description of his
personal experience. He had found the inner door
to Pure Being. The problem for the man now was
how to remain there.

On Saturday, Booker took the day off from work
and caught a bus that served the highway between
Taos and Santa Fe into the capital. Carlos had told
him about a rummage shop where he might buy
some inexpensive clothes. He purchased a pair of
blue dress pants, a white dress shirt, and a navy
blue blazer for $27 and two work shirts for another
$6. He could not resist a present for Nita. It was
a green crocheted tablecloth for $7.

Winn Conover, a clotheshorse since high school,

had never been near a second-hand clothing store. The idea of it would have been repulsive to him. Booker, however, considered the overfilled racks of coats and jackets, the narrow aisles, the boxes of shoes, and the tables piled high with pants and miscellaneous as a treasure-trove.

After a light lunch of tamales from a native vendor, Booker found his way to the Plaza and followed his curiosity into the historic buildings. At the Palace of the Governors, a guide showed the visitors the room where a Mexican Governor had the ears of Texan invaders nailed to his office wall. Joseph had not exaggerated the cruelty of the colonial period.

At the Museum of Fine Arts across the street, Booker was struck by the paintings of Georgia O'Keeffe. Her eye seemed to be a primal focus on the flowers and the stark and timeless moods of the desert.

Booker's most heartfelt discovery, however, was away from the Plaza at the small Loretto Chapel. The Sisters of Loretto were the first nuns to reside in Santa Fe. While building their chapel in 1873, the builders realized that the planned stairway to the choir loft would not fit, and they had no engineering solutions. A traveling master carpenter appeared and, with no drawings and crude tools, constructed an incredible spiral staircase with two complete 360-degree turns and no central support. Then the carpenter vanished without receiving payment. Booker sat for over an hour meditating on the beautiful and practical staircase as if he could make contact with the mysterious carpenter. If he had a wish, it would be to become such a man. Admiration for the expression of deep humility brought tears to his eyes.

That evening, when the chores were done at the pueblo, he ate supper with Nita, and they sat together at the fire as was their custom. Sometimes she would sing the prayers of her native tongue, but most of the time was spent in eyes-open silence. Booker had the idea that Nita was creating the space for his spiritual healing and nourishment. In these hours his awareness was keen, although his thoughts were few and had no direction. The time was seamless in warmth and satisfying comfort.

On Sunday, Booker rose before dawn, but ate no breakfast. He made the morning fire for Nita and then waited. Soon one of Joseph's clan priests came for him and led him to the sweat lodge roof. The fire below could be seen in flickering shadows at the sides of the hatch and in the smoky updraft. Booker helped the Indian men bring firewood to the roof and pass it down to the fire keeper throughout the morning. The four Indian men took their turns in the sweat lodge while the others huddled on the roof in silence. No introductions were made and no instructions given.

Booker felt it was near midday when Joseph climbed the ladder to the roof and the smoldering ashes of the fire were brought out in clay pots. Booker went down the ladder into the sweat room and found the smoke dissipated. A large pile of oval stones, heated since dawn, gave off an intense heat. Booker disrobed with the others as the ladder was set aside and the hatch closed. Water from a pottery bowl was spilled over the stones, making steam. The process was continued throughout the sweat to keep the lodge as hot as a good commercial steam room.

Joseph sang the prayer chants of his people, and with the intense heat, the effect was hypnotic. The fasting helped to induce dehydration, giving the body an internal focus and allowing the mind to float on the waves of heat and repetitious sound. For Booker, the result was deeper than the stillness he had achieved with breath control, but without effort.

As the body weakens and lessens its desires, there is the potential for clarity. Such is the case in the terminally ill who experience peace and happiness just prior to death. In the case of Booker and the Indian men, the state was induced. The hot, moist air of the sweat lodge entered the lungs and superheated the skin of the men. Their body temperatures went into the range of a fever. Delirium came and went, and in the spaces between were opportunities for visions.

Joseph had ceased to chant. There was only silence and great warmth. Each being reentered the experience of life before there was a body; before there was self-identification. Prior to the idea of self, there was Pure Being. Prior to the mind, there was existence. This is what the Creator made. All that followed was the invention of the mind, a layering over of the Creator's Reality. The mind created a substitute reality to account for its experience in the world. And the false reality grew as it was assigned name and meaning. And thus the separation continued until the individual created himself, and the Reality of God was replaced by the reality of man.

The sweat was a method to reverse the process and return an individual to the dimension of the Creator's Reality. It was an attempt to temporarily assassinate the mind and the body so that the pure being of spirit could emerge.

Booker's experience was a radical departure from what could be understood by the mind. The mind had no reference points to analyze or even to explain. The English word is "transcendent," but how can an individual, who appears to be present, exist apart from the material universe and explain himself?

Nita, Maria, and Pearl began the special meal to honor the men in the sweat lodge soon after they returned from church. Pearl cracked the corn on the coarsest of the three slanted metates stones which were cemented into square boxes of adobe on the floor. Maria then took the corn outside in a winnowing basket where she shook and swirled the corn to loosen the hulls and allow them to be carried off into the wind. The process continued until there was enough corn to be ground on the second stone, which reduced it to meal. Then the meal was worked on the third stone, almost slippery from use, until it was a fine corn flour.

The piki griddle was already in the fireplace. It was a smooth slab of soapstone, a very rare and precious find in Pueblo Indian territory. The stone was considered more valuable than all Nita's jewelry. It was an heirloom generations old.

Nita herself prepared the watery mixture of fresh corn flour and water. She worked the mush into a very specific consistency that only experienced piki makers could judge and held it in her right hand. Pearl tested the piki stone by pulling it from the fire, wiping it clean and sprinkling on drops of water. When the water rolled off the stone in sizzling balls, it was ready and brought to Nita. The difficult technique was to smear the dough over the surface of the hot griddle with the right hand and deftly peel the paper thin pancakes away with the left. Many fingers had been burned in vain attempts to learn the art of making piki bread. Nita was an acknowledged master. She worked in a rhythm dictated by the almost instantaneous cooking and soon had a stack of the thin sheets beside her. Pearl and Maria, who had apprenticed themselves to Nita and seen her make piki bread all their lives, smiled in appreciation as the old woman worked. Her withered and wrinkled hands performed an ageless dance over the revered stone that still pleased and amazed them.

For the feast, the piki bread would serve to wrap many choice meat and vegetable fillings prepared by Pearl and Maria. Nita had performed her magic and was served her favorite herbal tea and encouraged to watch the remainder of the preparation. Her only insistence was that the table be set with her new green crocheted tablecloth.

The feast following the sweat was as much a necessity as it was a ritual. The danger of dehydration to the point of coma and even death was a real possibility for the men enduring the sweat lodge. When the sweat was completed, some members might have to be pulled through the hatch on the roof by a sling arranged under their arms. Almost lifeless, they would be revived with sips of water and gradual cooling off in the open air. Then all the participants would drink and wash themselves to bring life back to the flesh. The meal which followed was the final restorative measure. Food, the communion symbol common to all peoples, would welcome them from death to life.

Booker was very weak and allowed himself to be assisted at the top of the ladder when he exited the sweat lodge. The men came out nearly naked and sat in a stupor on the roof as the two assistant priests who had waited for them brought water. Old Joseph smiled weakly to Booker in acknowledgment of their mutual survival.

"Did you have a vision?"

Booker nodded the affirmative.

"Good," Joseph said. "It was a good sweat."

Later, after they had washed and dressed, Booker walked in easy stride with Joseph as they crossed the plaza. "I do not understand my visions," Booker said.

"I am not surprised," Joseph said softly. "Everybody has been a Little Tail. That is what we say to the children who dance at the end of the Corn Dance line. In the beginning, we understand little."

"What does it mean when you see yourself as a deer running with other deer? Or feel like you are rain falling into a river and then flowing along its rapids? I extended my arms, and I was a tree where birds and squirrels made their home. And then I lay in a field, and when I raised my arms, they were stalks of ripe corn."

"You had these four visions?" Joseph asked.

"Yes," Booker replied.

Joseph stopped and motioned his priests and assistants to proceed. Then he turned to Booker. "Was there joy in these visions?"

"Great joy," Booker said.

The old man put his hands on Booker's shoulders as he looked into his face. "Then you are both the gift and the giver. You are at oneness with His creation. Four visions. Four is our holy number as there are four seasons and four stages of life. Four is the summing up. You are in the fourth stage of age, and you have had the four visions all righteous men seek for themselves. All the elements agree, you have achieved harmony with His creation. I am happy to be the witness."

"What do I do now?" Booker asked.

"Nothing," Joseph smiled. "You need do nothing. All things are accomplished."

"Then I will die?" Booker's question was childlike.

"No," Joseph laughed as he turned Booker's shoulder toward the Summer People. "First, you will eat piki bread."

CHAPTER FOURTEEN

On Monday at sunrise, Booker went to work with the Silvas as their regular helper. Once he had learned the skills of the job, there was little need for talk. Most of the time, except for a little singing by the father and son, they worked without speaking. It was a manner of the Indians that Booker appreciated.

The outdoor work, the non-fat diet, and the comforting evenings at the pueblo had given Booker a calm demeanor and a vigorously healthy body. He had lost his paunch to the extent that his cinched belt made folds in the waist of his first blue jeans. His weight loss might have been more were it not for the fact that he was increasing the muscle mass of his body significantly during the same period.

Booker's beard and mustache now required trimming. The desert sun bleached his head and facial hair into near whiteness. His natural hair color and the pepper in his beard were almost gone. Working beside the silver-haired Ernest, Booker could be taken for an Indian from a distance. Both men went to the same Indian barber, who cut their hair with scissors as they sat on a stool in the barber's back-yard. They bartered his services with firewood.

Booker found the simple routine of Indian life very satisfying. Although the Indians discussed the manners and qualities of the anglo among themselves in private, they never intruded on his psychological space with questions or petty conversations. The fact that Joseph had passed the word that Booker was his honored guest perhaps added additional sensitivity to the Indians' normal considerate customs.

It was during his second week of work with the Silvas that Booker discovered the money tucked into the pocket of a cleaned work shirt. The laundry for a second time appeared on his bed at midweek. It was a service Nita politely refused to acknowledge with anything other than a slight smile when Booker expressed his appreciation. As instructed by Maria, Booker had put ten dollars each night into a certain bowl displayed in the main room of Nita's house. The $120 in the shirt pocket appeared to be the same bills he had used to pay his room and board. Booker realized that he needed to discuss the matter with Maria before he said anything to Nita.

"This is Nita's way of saying that you are not a boarder. You are her guest," Maria explained.

"But can't she use the money?" Booker pleaded, feeling the weight of the gift.

"Our clan provides for her. She has everything she needs," Maria assured him.

"But my laundry and my meals," Booker persisted. "How can I repay her?"

Maria smiled with emotion and her eyes filled with tears. "You have given much more than you know."

The weeks that followed were days without number or disturbing incident. The daylight hours grew longer, and into July the temperature became very hot. The men worked until midmorning collecting wood, much of which would be brought back to the Silvas' yard to be stacked for winter customers. They also continued to supply the tourist restaurants with mesquite.

On Saturdays, Booker would go into Santa Fe or Taos to shop for his own needs and to bring back special treats for Nita. There was always something for her sweet tooth, plus a chicken or beefsteak and fresh vegetables for the week.

Sundays were spent with Joseph. Most of the summer living at the pueblo was done outdoors, so they walked in the early morning, drank tea and ate frybread, and then sat in the shade of the buildings receiving Joseph's priests and clan people who wished his counsel. Although Booker could not understand their language, he could sense a disruption in the stability of each supplicant's energy as a problem was laid before the cacique. Often there was a long silence before Joseph responded to what had been related. Booker did not need to be told that Joseph's chief function in these circumstances was healing. In some cases there was a great sense of relief and release after Joseph spoke. Booker felt that some kind of forgiveness had also been extended.

Joseph never offered an explanation to Booker about the nature of the problems presented or the process that followed. But at the end of such a day, when they ate their main meal as guests of an Indian family, Joseph took Booker's arm and said, "Your spirit was a great help today. Our best work was done in the silence."

Booker knew instinctively what the cacique meant. When the pueblo staged its annual Corn Dance to petition for rain for its crops, Booker sat with the Indian elders on benches outside an elaborate arbor built of branches and hung with beautiful blankets and embroideries. The arbor sheltered the figures of saints brought out from the pueblo church. The function of Booker and the old men was to keep the saints company. No one had to tell Booker that the Corn Dance was the most important Indian ritual of the year. The multitude of costumed participants was evidence enough.

On a Sunday in August, Booker sought Joseph's counsel for his own concern.

"There has been such profound peace here that I have fears about going into the world," Booker confided.

"Do you fear the temptation of women?" Joseph asked.

"I am aware that the body still has its urges, but it has not been a problem."

"Old age cures the sexual desire, but you must become very, very old to be completely free of it. It is a trip stone that will most often fell a man on the holy path. An old joke says that the final test of priesthood is to parade beautiful naked women in front of a line of naked priests and see what comes up."

Both men smiled and chuckled within their chests.

"In the world, sexual desire is used as a commercial tool to excite the people. In our country, it is ever present," Booker said.

"We observe these errors, and we see the effects on our young people. They turn their faces to this desire and worship it," Joseph said with regret.

"For me," Booker began, "it is anger that interrupts my peace. Even though I am withdrawn from television and other news of the world, I know that there is war, corrupt government, starvation, and cruel ignorance dominating the planet. It seems so unnecessary. The stupidity of it rises up in me. I remember the details of it, and my mind races away from my peace in anger."

"Yes, that is the conduct of the mind. It must be watched as an eagle follows a trout on the surface of a lake. Great attention is required. But what is the root cause? Is it really anger or is it fear?" The old priest raised his head to catch Booker's eyes.

"Fear?" Booker asked pensively.

"Follow the anger and see where it resides. Is it not fear, the Great Fear all human beings carry because they separated themselves from the Great Spirit? We deny Him and forever fear His judgment. We cannot abide this constant fear so we turn it outward onto our view of the world. We say that our neighbor has cheated us, or that we, ourselves, are unworthy of gifts. We become the judges of everything so that we might avoid His judgment. But He does not judge in the way we judge. He only loves. So we can choose His Love or our fear. The history of the world demonstrates which we have chosen."

"We have chosen our fear," Booker said in realization. "We have chosen separation."

"But He waits throughout eternity for us to choose again. That is the dimension of His Love."

"So my rebirth is the result of choosing Love over Fear." Booker paused to ponder what he had concluded. "To choose in every moment."

"In every moment," Joseph confirmed.

"I begin to understand what I have experienced," Booker said. "When the individual I identified as myself made judgments and decisions, I was fearful, angry, and unhappy. But when I gave up my investment in that identity and ceased to depend on my mind, I found peace."

"And yet you could travel, and work, laugh, find friendship. How is this possible?" The question was a teaching device. Joseph already knew the answer.

Booker was quiet for a while as he examined his thoughts. Then he smiled and looked into Joseph's expectant face. "You don't need the mind for much, do you?"

"You need the mind only to function in the performance of tasks. You never need the mind to have relationship. Choose the quiet mind of His Being and let that be the source of behavior." Joseph's eyes radiated joy as he shared his ultimate understanding with Booker. He had tried throughout his senior priesthood to articulate this truth to his own people, especially to his own priests, but he was not sure that any individual had made the connection from concept to experience. Finally, and with irony that the Great Spirit chose to further enlighten Joseph, the Indian cacique had fulfilled his function, not with a fellow Pueblo as he expected but with an anglo.

There was nothing more for the men to say to each other. They could rest in the complete satisfaction of their interconnection. In the graceful silence that followed, Booker had the persisting idea that he could find Truth in relationship with anyone. It would never be dependent on the appearance or attitude of the other. It would only require that he suspend judgment and see the seeming other as an extension of himself, a human being caught between Love and Fear, desperately seeking reunion and peace.

Joseph's contentment was mixed with the Great Spirit's humor. Just when Joseph considered that he knew the nature of His Creator, the Creator gave him a surprise. There was yet a speck of prejudice against the anglos to be healed. And the spiritual path was not always from understanding to experience. It could be reversed as in Booker's revelation. Joseph marveled at the scope of the Creator that no mind could contain.

CHAPTER FIFTEEN

The intensely bright summer passed into subdued September days. When the news arrived in an old pickup truck that had been sent to find them on the mesquite plains, Booker had no idea that he had been away from Norfolk for nearly four months. He had been living another life in an altered time, especially in Santa Fe. It was soon to end.

The young Indian driver gave the news quietly to Ernest after a wild, cloud-raising ride. Ernest removed his sweat-stained, broad-brimmed, western hat and thanked the boy with a solemn handshake. The boy waited and watched as the older man crossed to where Carlos and Booker stood in anticipation. Ernest addressed them both. "Chief Old Woman is gone," he said. "We will go home now."

The impact of what Ernest had said hung in the dry air and then was inhaled by Booker. The weight of it brought him to his knees, and when he exhaled the air that carried the news, a void sucked at his lungs until he felt hollow inside. It was a greater emptiness than when his own mother had died. It was loss without hope of replacement. He

wept, and the other men turned away in respect.
For them, Nita was a tribal icon, the greatest cultural treasurer of their clan. They knew that her life
would be celebrated around ritual campfires forever,
and that her spirit would continue to be a guide
to Pueblo women. In these ways, the Indians could
accept in stoicism her passing.

But Booker had no training or cultural experience in ancestor worship. All that he knew was
the immediate loss of his dearest relationship. At
that moment, grief separated him from spiritual
truth, and he was locked into the painful reality
of the world.

That morning Nita had embraced Booker and
kissed his cheek before he left the house. Although
she had touched his hand or shoulder with affection
before, the embrace of the morning seemed to be
a special recognition to Booker. Later, learning that
she had returned to her bed in the morning and
quietly died, he knew that her kiss had been a
goodbye. Maria told him that Nita had laid herself
on the bed and welcomed death without struggle or
discomfort. The expression on her face was serene.

Joseph was waiting for Booker when he returned
to the pueblo. Together with Ernest and Carlos, they
sat on the ground outside Nita's door. The Indian
men sang while the women went in to prepare the
body.

The burial of Nita, Chief Old Woman, was done
illegally and in secret. The Catholic clergy officiated
at the graveside in the Pueblo cemetery, but the coffin that was put in the ground did not contain the

deceased woman's body. It contained rocks wrapped in old blankets to approximate her weight.

On the day of her death, Pearl and Maria, assisted by the most senior women of their clan, dressed Nita's body in her best traditional dress and jewelry and collected the items she would need in the afterlife. She had told them exactly what she wanted. She wanted the bowl her mother had given to her as a child. She wanted two antique pottery jars filled with corn and pine nuts. She wanted an old wooden spoon and a ladle and her favorite willow bark basket. And finally, she asked for her best blanket and the green crocheted tablecloth.

As her most faithful grandchild, Pearl was to have the piki stone. Nita had survived all her own children. Maria, the faithful great-granddaughter, was to receive Nita's ceremonial rain sash among other items important to their native tradition. She would follow Pearl in the keeping of the tribal secrets.

While the women prepared the body, a party of clan priests carefully slipped away from their occupations and rendezvoused in the mountains above the pueblo. Posting a sentry to assure their privacy, they continued higher into the mountains along unmarked game trails until they reached a specific open-faced cave far off the path of public interest. At a known place on the cave floor, they removed flat stones concealing a deep rectangular hole completely lined with adobe bricks. The burial vault had been built by the priests who labored in secret for the sake of their ancestral shrine. In centuries past, the same adobe boxes had been used to store corn and wild seeds. Forgotten and discovered a hundred years later, the corn was still edible and, when planted, the wild seeds grew.

Today, the priests stacked the covering stones and prepared the area for the burial ceremony. Juniper sticks had to be collected for a campfire. When night came, they would serve as trail guides for the funeral party making its way up the dark path. There would not be many in the party. Joseph would lead, with two younger priests carrying a blanket litter containing the slight body of the Chief Old Woman. Her religious clan members, Pearl, Maria, and a few selected others would follow. It would be a hard climb for the old ones, perhaps three hours beyond the Pueblo cemetery.

One of the priests speculated to another while waiting at the cave that the anglo would be included in the funeral party.

"No," the second priest said in disbelief.

"Yes," the first contended. "I have sweated with this man. He is worthy."

"But he is not of the Deer Clan," the other refuted.

"Then tonight he will be," the senior man said with finality. "He is already being called Anglo Who Became Chief Old Woman's Son."

When the ceremony ended, these priests would seal the covering stones with wet adobe clay and then add a layer of cave dirt to further camouflage the grave. They would employ their skills to remove any traces of the campfire and any footprints or other scars in the environs which revealed human activity. Their work could not be completed until they made a daylight inspection of the gravesite and carefully worked their way down the obscure trails covering their tracks. They did these things as a sacred duty to prevent the sacrilege of their holy place.

The night was cool along the trail and the moon and stars were bright above the evergreen trees. Maria and Booker helped to support Pearl as they followed the inclined rocky path. It was after midnight when they finally reached the site. They rested while the campfire was lit well into the wide mouth of the cave. The glow of its illumination could be observed only from the direction of the cave opening. The smoke snaked along the cave roof and slithered away into the darkness. It was doubtful that the fire could be observed from the valley below.

When Pearl was rested and refreshed from the water jar, she and Maria saw to the laying out of the body and Nita's artifacts in the adobe pit. The Chief Old Woman was wrapped in her best blanket. A folded green crocheted tablecloth served as a pillow for her dark chiseled face and white hair.

Pearl lingered over the grave, making small adjustments in the positions of the eating bowl and the jars and the ladle until Maria gently pulled her away.

The ceremony was brief and quiet due to the proximity of civilization. A soft drumbeat accompanied some chanting and a shuffling dance as members of the funeral party passed close to the pit for final respects. Then Joseph spoke the eulogy in his tribal tongue and then in English.

"When the people went away from our religion and forgot our secrets and our rituals, Nita remained as an island in a flood. She was honored by her people as the Earth Mother who was the living example of our virtues. She will be remembered as long as there is a Deer Clan. She is one of the great spirits of our history, worthy of traditional burial to be a spirit guide in our ancestor worship. I say these things in the English language so that our brother, Anglo Who Became Chief Old Woman's Son, will know his spiritual Mother, and know that by her life, and her death, he becomes part of the Deer Clan."

Until that moment, Booker had remained strong in support of Pearl and Maria. He had held Pearl's arm on one side, with Maria on the other, as they had passed the four times by the grave in the ceremonial dance. But now he needed both Pearl and Maria to grip his arms and hold him as he trembled with emotion.

Joseph approached with a small decorated pottery jar into which he dipped his two forefingers and smeared deer's blood across Booker's forehead, down the bridge of his nose, and under both eyes. He performed the ritual while repeating a tribal incantation.

The way down the mountain in the dark required concentration for the sake of safety. Fatigued by both the climb and the spent emotions, the party's return to the pueblo was accomplished in a stupor.

For Booker, it was a blessed stupor. He did not have the resources to deal with a rampaging mind. Better it should remain in shock than inflict him with its pain.

When he had seen Maria and Pearl to their car, Booker wrapped himself in a blanket and sat outside Nita's door until it was time to walk to the highway and catch the Silvas' truck. He did not consider whether they would come or not. He did not consider eating. But the truck came, and Booker went to work. Ernest offered him morning coffee and frybread at the job, but did not mention the death of Nita until after lunch.

"We will quit early today," Ernest said. "There is a church funeral at four o'clock."

Ernest and Carlos dropped Booker at the head of the road to the pueblo as usual and then went home to collect their wives and change their clothes. There was a sizable crowd for the Catholic funeral, but Booker did not join them. He observed from the edge of the village. Joseph and two of the priests who had sweated with Booker found him and stood silently by. They did not intrude with talk. They rather stood like trees, leaning in sympathetic harmony against the storm, giving shelter and strength to each other.

CHAPTER SIXTEEN

On the morning after the Catholic funeral, Booker found Pearl at Nita's place by the fire, preparing his breakfast. There was a momentary shock at seeing the old woman, but he knew better than to question her. After she served him, Pearl explained. "You may stay in this house as long as you wish. Sometimes Maria and I will come to cook for you. We will do your laundry."

"It is not necessary," Booker offered.

"You are our clan brother," she smiled. "We do these things to please ourselves."

"I do not know if I will stay," Booker said.

"See Joseph," Pearl advised. "He will have another house for you if you prefer."

"I love this house," he replied.

Pearl took his hand like an elder sister. "I know," she said.

For the rest of the week, Indian women brought prepared dishes to the house the way friends do for a family in bereavement. Booker ate only to sustain himself. The struggle with his own grief had opened the door to the grief his disappearance might have generated in Norfolk. He could not escape the consequences that his continued abandonment would cause. The telegram to Ellen was supposed to be temporary. In view of the months which had passed, it now seemed extremely insufficient.

The temptation was to remain at the pueblo. The loss of Nita hopefully would heal. The Deer Clan had offered him a permanent home, isolated from the world he had rejected. He could practice peace among ancient Indian monuments with Joseph as his elder brother and Pearl and Maria as his sisters.

Yet there was another family which bound him to a former existence. There would always be an incompleteness deep within him until it was healed. Booker realized that his function was forgiveness. But how was he to begin? What could he say to Ellen? How could he explain his actions to Theo and Buffy? How could he respond to the name Winston Conover when he was no longer the same man? How could he say to his family, "Your husband, your father died and was resurrected as Booker Washington Jones"?

On Sunday, seated outside with their backs against an adobe wall of the Winter People, Booker posed these questions to Joseph. Joseph was quiet for some time before he spoke. "It is difficult for the family to accept the father as a holy man. Even among our people, it is so. The family remembers the former man who served them. Now he says that he serves another Master, and they have feelings of betrayal. They are angry, and they try to break the holy man's heart so that they can possess him again. Sometimes they succeed."

"I don't know if I can risk my peace," Booker admitted.

"Is your peace complete while you feel obligation?" Joseph spoke with his eyes unfocused, his back erect and his body very still as if listening to the wind.

"No," Booker said. "Old habits of the mind linger to surprise me like a rattlesnake among the mesquite."

Joseph smiled and said, "You are painting images like an Indian."

"I can see no solution to the problems in Norfolk," Booker lamented.

"Who is seeing the problems, and who is seeing the lack of a solution?" Joseph asked.

"I am," Booker affirmed.

"Get in touch with that I," Joseph advised.

"That I is Winn Conover," Booker realized.

Joseph remained quiet as Booker remade the connection that his peace had never been achieved within the mind of Winn Conover. Had he forgotten? It was a constant imperative to remember. He was not the body or the mind that sought so strongly to be identified and acknowledged. And with that realized, Booker relaxed into the place where thoughts did not abide and where all solutions were possible.

Joseph sensed the shift in awareness of his spirit brother and posed the question, "Now what does the spirit of your heart say to do?"

"To return to Norfolk," Booker said.

"For what purpose?" Joseph continued.

"Healing," Booker answered.

"Make no plans," Joseph advised. "Be as empty as a water jar left in the desert. Let them pour onto you their anger, their guilt, and their suffering. Reside in the spiritual heart and these black waters will evaporate and rise to become white clouds against the blue sky of a new day. And in the new day, they will feel your warmth like a gentle sun."

"Will they forgive me?" Booker asked.

"Who is it who is in need of forgiveness? Let him first forgive, and then see if the need arises."

"I will write a letter and then talk to Ellen on the telephone to prepare them," Booker said.

Joseph did not respond. There were hawks circling above the mountains on updrafts of warm air rising off the valley floor. They were not seeking prey. They were riding the air currents as an unobserved child might dance because its nature was to celebrate. Joseph wanted to project himself upward and fly with the hawks, but he was bound to the ground by the trial he foresaw for his spirit brother. There was the danger of loss. Joseph had seen men of spirit pulled back into the world. There was little more he could do to prepare Booker for the test. He could only pray that Anglo Who Became Chief Old Woman's Son would survive.

That evening, Booker wrote the letter to Ellen on tablet paper and a pencil provided by one of the Indian shopkeepers. The letter began, "Since the telegram I sent you in May, I lost track of time while practicing spiritual contemplation. It was necessary for me to find meaning and purpose to my life. I regret that the radical nature of this process was so hard on you and the children. I hope we can share what I have discovered. I would like to come back to Norfolk to heal the hurts I have caused. I will telephone you at the house on Saturday about noon your time. I have enough money to fly into Norfolk if that is suitable for you. I can come as soon as you agree. I love you and Theo and Buffy and want you to be happy."

On Monday morning, the job with the Silvas took the workmen to Taos. Booker asked Ernest to stop at the post office where he purchased an envelope and posted the letter to Norfolk. Since he did not know the mailing address of his pueblo, he could not include a return address. The first class letter would take at least three days to be delivered.

Saturday morning, Booker took the bus into Santa Fe and looked for a public phone booth that afforded some privacy. He found it off the lobby of La Fonda, a large tourist hotel on the Plaza. Despite his prayerful preparation, the call was difficult to initiate. He paced the lobby, giving glances to a wall clock as the hour approached. In his best jeans and western shirt and his newest purchases from the thrift store, a pair of used, but formerly expensive, western boots and a brown, broad-brimmed western hat, the well conditioned, white-bearded older man could have been mistaken for one of the Canyon Road painters or sculptors.

When Booker finally took a seat in the telephone booth and closed the door, he remembered that he did not have enough change to sustain a long conversation. Then too, he did not want interruptions from a long distance operator who might break in with demands for more coin deposits. The solution was to make the call collect. When the mechanical voice asked the name of the caller, Booker had to remember to use the name Ellen would recognize. Suddenly, she was on the line.

"Winn, is it really you?"

"Yes," he said.

"The postmark said Taos, New Mexico. Are you in New Mexico?" Ellen seemed to be shouting as if she needed to increase the volume of her voice to compensate for the distance.

"I'm calling from Santa Fe," he said calmly.

"Do you realize the heartbreak you have caused us? Theo and Buffy are here. We are very upset."

"That is why I am calling," Booker said as Winn. "I want to heal that condition."

"After four months," she accused. "You call after four months and expect everything to be normal?"

"I have no expectations," Booker said. "Tell me what you want me to do."

"I wish you had died," Ellen cried out bitterly and then started to weep uncontrollably.

Booker could hear Buffy consoling her mother, and then Theo recovered the dropped phone.

"Dad? It's Theo. Things have been pretty rough around here with the police and the publicity. Just when we were recovering, Mom got your letter. She is not handling it very well."

"I understand," Booker said. "How are you doing?"

"I'm relieved that you are not murdered, but I

can't justify what you did. You put us through hell."

"What if I told you that it was necessary," Booker said.

"I would say bullshit. I don't want to hear that kind of crap."

"All right, Theo. I can understand why you might feel that way. What can I do to make you feel better?"

"Jesus. I don't know. We're doing pretty good without you, frankly. I came back from Vermont to support Mother and help with the business. I picked up your commercial listings, and I have made five big sales since you left."

"That's fine," Booker said without the resentment Theo had intended to inflict with his boast. "You should be able to make a profitable career for yourself."

"I intend to. Mother has promised me a partnership."

"That seems appropriate," Booker said. The effect was to take the conflict out of Theo's proclamation.

Theo then seemed at a loss for words and retreated. "Buffy wants to talk to you."

"Daddy," Buffy began breathlessly. "The reason we are so upset is because we didn't think that the damn telegram was from you. We thought, and the police thought, it was just another crazy person trying to torment Mother. You wouldn't believe all the crazy mail we have been getting. Mother is so embarrassed. She can hardly show houses. People can be so cruel. They want to know what she did to drive you away, that is if you weren't kidnapped and murdered. Oh my god, we'll be on the front pages again if you come home."

"Do you want me to come home?" Booker asked as Buffy paused to take a breath.

"Of course we do. Well, I do. Mother doesn't know what she wants to do. She does so well, and then when you think she is superwoman, she falls apart. The attorneys are around her like vultures. They want her to file for divorce, to file for probate. And the damn police are worse. They don't want us to file for anything. They just want us to go away."

"I can see that it has been horrible for you," Booker concurred.

"It *has* been horrible, Daddy. Are you all right? Your letter was kind of mystical. Did you join a cult or something?"

"I'm fine, and I didn't join a cult. I joined an Indian clan."

"You are kidding me?" Buffy asked with exaggeration.

"Actually, I'm not. I had a very profound experience among the Pueblo Indians around Santa Fe."

"Oh God, this is strange," Buffy said in amazement. Then Booker could hear her interrupted by Ellen and Theo, and Buffy's response to their questions. "Daddy joined the Indians in New Mexico." More unintelligible questions. "Well, that's what he said." Then Buffy redirected herself to her father. "Hello, Daddy? We've got lots of questions."

"Yes, I suppose you have. And I have answers."

"He says he has answers," Buffy said away from the phone.

Theo then took the phone from his younger sister. "If you come home, we'll have to tell the cops."

"Can't that be done quietly without alerting the media?" Booker asked.

"I suppose so," Theo negotiated. "When would you come?"

"As soon as your mother was ready," Booker said.

"You would have to stay with Buffy," Theo advised. "Mom is not ready to have you back in the house."

"That's understandable," Booker replied.

"You want me to pick you up at the airport?"

"That would be helpful."

"Do you need any money?" Theo asked.

"No, thank you. I'll have to call you when I have a flight."

"Call me at the office. If I am not there, you can leave the details on my voice mail. Don't worry, I'll be there whenever you arrive."

"I trust you, and I am grateful," Booker responded. "Does your mother want to talk to me again?"

"No," Theo said, making his own decision. "I think it best that we give her time to adjust. You can see her when you get here."

There being an awkward silence, Booker concluded the call. "I'll see you soon."

"OK, Dad," Theo responded. "We'll see you."

The connection went dead, and Booker sat in the booth holding the silent phone in his lap until a stranger tapped on the glass door to request its use.

CHAPTER SEVENTEEN

Saying goodbye to the Sangre de Cristo Mountains at Santa Fe was not easy for Booker. If there was a sacred place on the planet for him, it would be high among these ridges along the unmarked trails that led to a certain cave. He had made the climb once more to sit with Joseph at the feet of Nita, his spirit guide, his Indian Mother. It had been a gathering of strength for what he knew must be done. And then, too compressed in time, Ernest Silva was driving him to the airport in Albuquerque in wordless, deep companionship.

"Sing the song of collecting firewood," Booker requested. And the silver-haired Indian sang most of the way down Interstate 25.

In parting at the curb of the airport departure terminal, Ernest took Booker's hand and said, "I will teach you this song when you return, and we will sing until all the jackrabbits have run from the mesquite."

"We will sing," Booker promised.

"And then we will eat a jackrabbit stew, and Pearl will make piki bread."

"Yes," Booker confirmed. "I will dream of piki bread."

Booker had money for a one-way ticket to Norfolk, with enough left over to cover two days at a
truck stop. He did not consider Winn Conover's resources as something that was available to Booker
Jones. Booker Jones was prepared to be self-sufficient although he had learned to accept the gifts of
others. He was content to perform a modest function to meet his necessities. Booker knew that there
was little happiness in excessive activity. No ambition, nor the drive to succeed, remained in him. And
yet, he did not see himself as an ascetic, or a
priest. Remaining at the source of inner peace still
required effort.

Theo was nervously waiting at the arrival gate
when his father's flight taxied into position. He had
previewed in his mind a dozen scenarios of how
they would greet each other and what they would
say. Rather than an immediate encounter, Theo decided to watch the passengers exit from a distance
so that his approach could be more considered.

As the passengers exited the ramp into the terminal, Theo looked intently for a man he could recognize as his father. No one fit his expectations.
After the last passenger emerged, Theo moved to
the head of the gate and peered down the tunnel-
like ramp.

"Son of a bitch," he hissed out loud in anger.
When he turned, intending to stalk out of the airport in justifiable rage, he found a white-bearded
cowboy in his path.

"Excuse me," he said in forced politeness as he
attempted to walk around the man.

"Theo," the man said.

Theo stopped abruptly and turned toward the old cowboy who was just removing his broad-brimmed hat.

"Maybe I should have worn my suit and shaved," the cowboy said. "I didn't think."

"My God," Theo was flabbergasted. "Dad? Is that you?"

"That's a profound question, but I guess from your point of view, I'd have to say, yes, it's me."

Theo extended his arms with open palms to show bewilderment, "What happened to you?"

"I lost thirty pounds," Booker offered.

"Your hair," Theo blurted out. "It's white."

"I've been working outdoors in the desert," Booker explained. "I guess the sun and the piñon smoke from the fireplace gave me a bleach job."

"You look so different. I didn't recognize you."

"That's understandable," Booker said. "How are your mother and Buffy?"

"Mother is still in shock. Buffy is fixing up a room for you at her house."

"When can I see your mother?" Booker asked.

"Tomorrow," Theo replied. "I'll have to prepare her for your new appearance. She packed a suitcase for you in case you needed clothes or your shaving kit."

"I have everything that I need," Booker said, indicating the backpack at his feet.

"That's it?" Theo questioned.

Booker confirmed with a nod of his head and picked up the backpack.

"Then I guess we can go," Theo said. "I'm driving your Explorer. I guess you will want it back."

"No," Booker said as they walked through the terminal. "I don't drive. Why don't you keep it."

"Really?" Theo said with his first enthusiasm. "For keeps?"

"Sure," Booker confirmed.

"How will you get to the office?" Theo inquired.

"I won't be working at the office," Booker said simply.

Theo allowed the statement to stand without clarification. He did not want to compromise the possibility of his own advancement.

The ride from Norfolk International Airport via I-64 to the Virginia Beach suburbs took about half an hour. Booker answered the questions Theo posed out of curiosity: How did his father find clothing that night? How had he traveled and supported himself all the way to New Mexico? Booker related the simple outline without detail or embellishment. He did not include any spiritual aspects of his relationship to the Deer Clan.

The question of "why" was deferred until the family could be together.

Buffy cried when she saw her father get out of the car. She had no reservations about running down the walkway to greet him with a long hug and kisses on his forehead.

"You look like you just stepped out of a western movie," she said. "How did Theo recognize you?"

"I didn't," Theo offered as he lifted his father's backpack.

"Bill is at the lumber yard," Buffy said, referring to her husband, who worked in his family-owned building supply business. "I wanted to see you alone first."

At the kitchen table over coffee, Booker was made to recount what he had previously told Theo, with the addition of more details to satisfy Buffy.

"I can't believe they had no indoor toilet," Buffy said. "It's like you were living in the pages of *National Geographic*. And I don't know how you got up to catch the firewood truck at sunrise when Momma could never get you going in the morning before eight o'clock."

"I'm a different person," Booker tried to tell them. "I still get up before dawn. I hope that won't disturb you."

"What in the world will you do that early?" Buffy asked.

"I can take a walk to see the sun come up. I can make breakfast for myself."

"You will have to get breakfast for yourself if you are up that early," Buffy said in half jest. "Bill and I don't have to be to work until nine. Most mornings, it's coffee and a bagel while we're watching the weather channel and then we're out the door on the run."

"I think it was Thomas Jefferson who said that he never wanted the rising sun to catch him in bed," Booker recalled.

"If that's what they taught you at UVA, Dad," Theo tested, "how come you didn't start getting up early until a few months ago?"

"I'm a slow learner," Booker admitted. It made them laugh for the first time since his return.

Before Bill came home, Theo left to take his ob-
servations to his mother. He had made a brief telephone call to her when they arrived at Buffy's, and
Buffy herself would be on the phone later that
night for over an hour, detailing her point of view.
Thus Ellen would be brought up to date on the
delinquent adventures of her husband.

Ellen could not make up her mind if she would
greet Winn with a jubilant embrace or a slap in
the face. Her mind was as split as she imagined
his personality to be. If Winn had been nothing
else in their marriage, he had been reliable, dependable. He was a man of good character who
had never given her cause to doubt his love or
devotion. Even in the hardest years of their business, when the stress of working together day
after day drove them apart, she trusted that their
relationship would endure.

And it did. Through the disappointments with
the children, into middle age, it endured. If there
were reservations, Ellen thought that they were at
least normal. Most people of their age and class
were sedate, even bored with their lives. The fun
she seemed to remember from earlier years was
something that now had to be manufactured by exotic vacations. Sexual excitement was reduced to the
vicarious experience of romance novels and a soap
opera Ellen taped for playback every weekday. At
worst, she judged that her marriage was stale. It was
something women in her position joked about and
secretly feared when they learned that one of their
peers was being divorced for a younger woman.

Even without another woman, Ellen deeply resented her husband's sudden abandonment. It was so unexpected, so uncharacteristic of the man she thought she knew intimately. He had broken the covenant of trust with her. He had destroyed her illusions of permanence and emotional comfort. For these things, she was unprepared to forgive him.

On the other hand, she could rationalize the entire humiliating incident if he had become mentally unstable. A mini-stroke could have altered Winn to the point of his wandering off in amnesia. Or he might have suffered a chemical imbalance. Parkinson's Disease! Viral infection! Carbon monoxide poisoning! Any rational excuse that would spare her from personal rejection would be welcomed.

The news from Theo and Buffy was confusing. Their father seemed rational, but he was obviously changed. He retained a sense of humor, but he didn't talk the same way they remembered. He could respond to questions with direct answers, but he didn't elaborate as he had formerly done. Both of the children noticed the absence of his two facial idiosyncrasies.

"Mother," Buffy had described on the phone, "it's like on Star Trek when the aliens take control of Captain Kirk. He looks like the Captain, but Spock is suspicious. You know what I mean? It's Daddy, but it's different from Daddy."

Theo had a different kind of observation. "He told me to keep the Explorer. Now when did Dad give anything like that away? He might let me have the car below blue book and let me make payments at no interest, but he wouldn't just give it to me. It goes against his work ethic. How many times have I heard that lecture: You don't appreciate what you don't earn. And another thing. Buffy offered Dad a beer, his brand, and he turned it down. When have you ever known Dad to turn down a beer?"

The consensus among them was to wait for Winn's further explanation before taking action. Perhaps they could get him to a doctor.

Ellen would depend on her prescription tranquilizers to make it to the noon reunion. It would not be the worst day of her life. That had already occurred in May.

CHAPTER EIGHTEEN

Bill and Buffy Mason lived off Little Neck
Road in a well established Virginia Beach neighborhood. The really expensive properties with their boat
docks on the Lynnhaven Bay were a few blocks
away. Since Little Neck Road bisected a peninsula
which dead-ended at the Lynnhaven, there was no
through traffic. The way was lined with pine trees
and dogwoods. The still-green lawns were accented
with large azalea and camellia bushes which would
produce huge blossoms of pinks and crimsons and
violets in early April. The color in the house-front
gardens this time of year was mostly from pansies,
chrysanthemums, and an occasional Flowering Senna.
When Booker began his nearly-two-mile walk from
Buffy's house to the heavily commercial Virginia
Beach Boulevard, the sky was still dark. The sunrise
was very gradual, revealing the floral opulence as a
shy woman might reveal her beauty. The allure was
not lost on Booker.

At the head of the road, there was a strip shopping center that included a twenty-four-hour supermarket. Early Sunday morning in affluent Virginia
Beach, there were few shoppers. Booker found the

items that he needed for breakfast and went to the only open check-out register, where a young clerk and the night manager were talking. Booker was wearing the same clothes he had worn the previous day, including his western hat.

"You are either up very early, or you line danced all night," the manager said in the way of a greeting.

"Up early," Booker responded with a smile. "I like to see the sun come up."

"You live around here?" the manager asked as the clerk rang up the groceries.

"I'm staying up on Little Neck with my daughter and son-in-law for a while. By the way, do you need any help? I'm looking for work."

"What can you do?" the manager asked out of politeness.

"Well, I've had some recent experience unloading trucks," Booker answered.

"You are hitting me right where I live," the manager admitted. "As night manager, it's my responsibility to accept deliveries and restock our inventories. The traffic is so bad on the boulevard that the big trucks want to unload between five and seven in the morning, and then I've got to get the stuff off the docks and into stock. Do you know how many volunteers you can get to unload trucks at five o'clock in the morning?"

"You can get me," Booker offered.

The manager laughed and extended his hand. "My name is Wilson James. Can you start tomorrow morning?"

"I'm Booker Jones, and yes, I can."

The night manager bagged Booker's groceries and walked with him away from the register so that he could discuss terms.

"I can use you from five to eight every day and pay you cash out of our casual labor fund. How about ten dollars an hour?"

"That's fine," Booker agreed.

"If you are dependable and do a good job, I could give you extra work in the back of the store and up front as a relief bagger," James said. "Of course, those are minimum wage jobs."

"I understand," Booker said. "I'm happy to do whatever you need."

"I like to employ seniors," James confided. "Kids these days don't want to work hard, and you can never depend on them."

"And yet all of them are our children," Booker responded.

James seemed confused for a moment and then said, "Oh, yea, like we are all children of God. I forgot it was Sunday."

Bill came downstairs to the kitchen just after nine. It was his only day off that week, so he slept late. He was surprised to find his father-in-law at the stove ready to serve him breakfast.

"Should we wait for Buffy?" Booker asked.

"No," Bill said. "She's washing and setting her hair."

Booker served Bill the same breakfast he had eaten earlier: grits with stewed fruit and herbal tea.

"This is perfect," Bill said when he was served.

"Ellen will have a big dinner for us so we need to eat light."

When Buffy came down, her father served her. Although it was not the French Toast specialty he had prepared for her as a child, the new tastes were enjoyable.

The morning passed as easily as walking a tight-rope can be managed. The main objective was not to look down.

Booker took a shower and put on his second-hand blue suit, white shirt, and western boots. Buffy remarked how good he looked, so trim, even distinguished.

The ride to Norfolk was along a familiar route. Bill and Buffy made innocuous comments to fill the vacuum of impending emotions, but they became more and more uncomfortable as they neared Lake-wood.

Booker Jones as Winn was not at the effect of their approach-avoidance conflict. His disciplined mind was quiet. While the players in the noon drama wrote and rewrote their scripts against the frantic deadline, Booker had the freedom of an audience member. He had no lines to memorize, no poses to strike. He was free to be himself, to be spontaneous from a well of deep compassion. He was content not to be the doer in any plot that developed. This was his constant prayer.

Ellen had considered having the Sunday dinner catered, but she needed the occupation of cooking. Before the children were teenagers, the Sunday dinner after a Baptist church service had been a Conover tradition. Ellen could manage the southern fare of a baked chicken or beef roast with peas or green beans, creamed potatoes or baked sweet potatoes, a tomato and iceberg lettuce salad, iced tea or coffee, and a chocolate cake for dessert. Today it would be a chuck roast cooked in the oven with onions and carrots. There would be creamed potatoes for the gravy and baby green peas. It was selected consciously as Winn's favorite Sunday dinner. If the meal and the chocolate layer cake did not speak to their life together, nothing would.

Ellen had completed her kitchen work, put away her apron, and refreshed her hair and make-up in anticipation of the noon hour. Theo joined his mother early, as promised, and made himself a drink with his father's best bourbon. The morning hours had been very tense for him.

Ellen did not greet her husband at the front door, but waited in the space of their seldom used formal living room. The dogs had been put in the garage to simplify the event. Booker entered the room and stopped six feet away so as to yield to Ellen the right of initiative. She made her decision and came tearfully to embrace him. They held each other for several minutes. The only sound in the room was Ellen's sobbing. Booker patted her back to soothe her and whispered four times that he was sorry. Then she looked into his clear brown eyes, saw compassion, and kissed him on the lips.

The dinner was awkward. Buffy helped her mother finish and serve the meal which was praised three or four times beyond propriety. Bill contributed

news about new housing starts in the Tidewater
area, Buffy described her Daddy's surprise breakfast,
and Theo gave an update on local events of the
past few months. There was an obvious détente concerning the cause célèbre.

But finally, with second cups of coffee taken into
the family room with its view of the Lafayette
River, all eyes turned to Booker as Winn for the
denouement. He began without any preconceived
idea on what he would say. It was not the kind of
after-dinner speech that required special acknowledg-
ments. There was no danger of losing his audience
by their inattention.

"I have learned that there are two ways toward
understanding anything. One is verbal and relies on
experience and intellect, and the other is nonverbal,
a total stillness of the mind. I am asking you to
use both methods in hearing me out today. The
most important elements of what has happened to
me cannot be explained to the rational mind. I cannot even satisfy myself with the story, so I know
that it will be very difficult for you. But if you can
suspend judgment, and join me in the quiet place
of the heart, you can be a part of my experience."

"I've never heard you talk this way," Ellen said.

"It sounds like new age religion to me," Theo accused.

"Daddy is not new age, are you Daddy?" Buffy
asked.

"It's new to me, but a man I know in New Mexico says that his people have had these experiences
for thousands of years. All I know is the Bible. I

need to reread the New Testament, but I think what I experienced is what Jesus was trying to teach his disciples."

"So it is religious," Ellen confirmed. "Did one of those preachers on television get to you? Did you read some radical book? Is that why you walked out on us? Is that what's to blame?"

"No one is to blame," Booker said. "No one drove me away or seduced me away. Before we go any further, it would help me if we can be silent for a few minutes. Let's allow the stress of the day to fall away and clear our minds so that we can start fresh and relaxed."

"Like meditation," Buffy offered.

"Sounds like the start of a prayer meeting," Theo said as a sarcastic aside.

"Let's cooperate with your father," Ellen said to her children. "The sooner we get through this, the better."

The silent minutes were much easier for Booker than they were for the others. Ellen closed her eyes and tried to pray without success. Buffy remembered that she had some grocery shopping to do and tried to recall the items that she needed. Theo kept opening his eyes to observe the others as well as his wristwatch. When he glanced at his father's unguarded meekness, he saw him as a pathetic vestige of what he had been as the head of the family business. Theo had recently spoken to his father with a disrespect he never would have attempted before the disappearance. Theo's challenges met with no counterattack as he might have expected.

His father did not even defend himself. The void brought out a cruel assertiveness that was more common among boys on a combative playing field than it was between traditional sons and their fathers. The family crisis had afforded Theo the power of righteous indignation, and he exercised it.

Although Booker sensed that the only quiet mind in the room had been his own, he began again the process of healing.

"More than a year ago, I began a serious review and inventory of my life. I had a happy, stable childhood, a good education, an excellent marriage blessed with two healthy children, a successful career, and a business with my wife that placed us in the top one or two percent of wealth and power in the world. I had achieved everything I had hoped for as a young adult, but something was missing. It was not material. It was not being mid-fifty and overweight. It was deeper. And it was not outside of myself, it was somewhere inside."

"Everyone feels that way at our age," Ellen interjected. "That's why psychiatrists live in mansions and drive BMWs."

"Yes," Booker agreed. "Every individual senses that there is something more to life, but I wanted desperately to find it. I had the intense feeling that it was a place that I could reach if I just tried hard enough. One night, I realized that I was not my own body. It frightened me terribly. I thought that I would die. It was like stepping out of my body and seeing that I was not bound to it."

"Why didn't you tell me?" Ellen asked.

"I thought I might be going crazy, or that it was a dream," Booker said. "If the body was not the essence of what I was, I turned to my mind. I watched it with all my energy. And the more intently I watched it, the slower the thoughts developed. I could actually see them one at a time bubble to the surface of my awareness. At the office or out making a sales call, my mind was racing at a hundred miles an hour. Normally, it was completely out of control. But when I focused my attention on it, I could slow it down. If I held my breath, I could put the brakes on it in a minute. It was wonderful. It made the days more comfortable, more relaxed. At night, I began to spend hours slowing down my mind. Ten miles an hour. Five miles an hour. Less than a mile an hour. Dead stop. No thoughts. And there was something there. Something beyond my mind. It was the place I had been longing for. It was absolutely peaceful. It was beyond description. Right there inside of me. All the time, it was right there. I realized that finding this place was the purpose of life. Nothing else really mattered. But it was very difficult to remain there. The high state of concentration would lapse into beautiful dreamless sleep. But then the morning would come, and the consciousness would reemerge with its mental agenda, and I would be back to my troubled self. Heaven was a temporary state, but at least I knew that I could get there. I lost any ambition for anything other than this place of complete happiness. Somewhere in this process I got the mad idea that I had to renounce my existence as

Winn Conover and somehow remake myself into a man who could function in the world while at the same time remaining in the holy place. The morning I left was totally unplanned. I had no idea where I would go or what I would do. I had stopped thinking for the most part."

"So you did leave the house buck naked?" Buffy asked.

"Yes, I did."

"If we had this story on tape, we could probably use it to have you committed within twenty-four hours," Theo observed.

"Will you see a psychiatrist?" Ellen asked. "People will understand if we say that you were temporarily insane."

Booker smiled. "I'm still insane."

"You've had a breakdown, Honey. All you need is rest and medication."

"I will see doctors if that will help you," Booker said, "but my condition is not medical."

"Why don't we let the experts decide," Theo asserted.

Booker as Winn did not attempt to explain himself further, but agreed to do what they wanted. He kissed his crying wife goodbye when he left with Buffy and Bill. No one seemed to want him back in Lakewood.

CHAPTER NINETEEN

Monday morning, Booker returned from his unloading labors and the four-mile round trip walk to greet Bill and Buffy as they were about to leave the house.

"There is food in the fridge, and you know how to reach me at work," Buffy advised. "Mother is calling a few of your friends and letting them know where you are. It might be good for you to play golf or something."

Buffy was the office manager at Dax Cable TV and supervised a sizable staff of telephone and counter service personnel. If she had not developed a prejudice against it, she might have been a good real estate salesperson. But Buffy had decided as a teenager that she wanted a nine-to-five job where nobody could call her at home demanding to be shown a house.

At twenty-three, although she had left college to marry Bill, she felt very satisfied with her life. She would tell anyone who asked that she and Bill were planning no family until they had vacationed on five continents. The score was already up to three.

Booker would initiate no telephone calls, but he would answer the phone as a courtesy to the caller. Ellen called shortly after Booker had gotten out of the shower. She asked if he wanted to come to the office and got a polite negative. She told him that Theo would be calling him about his medical appointments as soon as they were arranged. Did he want anything from the house? Did he need any money?

"Sid Taylor is in Bayside Hospital. I didn't want to tell you first thing. Remember, he was having tests before you left. Well, it's cancer. He is going downhill fast. I thought you should know."

Sid and Bessie Taylor had been social friends of the Conover's for over twenty-five years. Sid had Lawyer's Title Insurance and a real estate appraisal business so they had often worked together to mutual benefit. Sid and Bessie had a Hatteras sport fishing boat at Rudy Inlet. They loved deep sea fishing and had shared their passion with Ellen and Winn on many happy excursions.

Sid liked to tease Winn about the price of the fish that they caught. "If you add up the cost and upkeep of the boat, the fuel, the tackle, and the booze and divide the total by the number of fish caught, it comes out to about $500 a fish."

"You need to get out more often," Winn would counter.

"One of these days," Sid would say, "I'm going to sell my business and become a charter boat captain. I'll fish every damn day the weather doesn't keep us tied to the dock."

Booker took a cab to Bayside Hospital and found his way to the oncology wing. He ran into Bessie in the hall outside Sid's room.

"My God, Winn, is it you?"

After an almost desperate embrace, Bessie stepped back with one hand maintaining contact with Booker. "Ellen said you dressed like a cowboy. Are you all right?"

"I'm fine. How is Sid?"

Bessie pulled Booker close to the wall and spoke in lower, intense tones. "You better prepare yourself. He has lost a lot of weight and the radiation treatments aren't helping. He won't eat. He wants to go home, but I can't take care of him there. The doctors don't give us much hope."

"How is his spirit?" Booker asked.

"Oh, he's down, Winn. He's angry at everybody. He knows that he is dying, but he can't accept it. The pain medication makes him sleep a lot. But he'd love to see you, Winn. His other friends have stopped coming. They can't take seeing him like this. He is a shell of what he was. Prepare yourself for a shock. I know he can see it on our faces, but what are we to do?"

Booker held the grieving wife in his arms and poured out a deep compassion that had no basis in circumstance. It required no words or definition. Bessie ceased to shutter and succumbed to its warmth.

"It seems like a miracle that you are here," she finally said. "Ellen said that you were different. You are. You are warmer, stronger."

Inside the room, Bessie stood by the bed and encouraged her husband to return to consciousness. "Look who's here, Baby. It's Winn."

Sid Taylor blinked and moved uncomfortably on his pillow. Booker stepped into view and took the hand which lay limp at Sid's side.

"My God, Winn. You came home," Sid said weakly.

"I came back for the fishing," Booker said with a broad smile.

"Take my Hatteras out and sink it with me tied to the fighting chair," Sid said through clenched teeth.

"That's the Viking way, isn't it?" Booker asked.

"That's my way," Sid said with some effort required. "Damn it, Winn. I don't want to die like this." His eyes cut to the stand from which his IV bags hung. Then he looked down to his waist and complained in a voice near tears, "I'm catheterized." The final syllables slurred.

Booker stepped closer and leaned in so that he could meet his friend's eyes. "It's just your body, Sid. There is a lot more to you than that. Life is not a blue marlin you can fight and break and bring to the boat as a trophy. Life is the biggest marlin you ever heard about. But you don't catch him, you ride him in the ocean forever."

"They told me you were crazy," Sid said. "But I like crazy."

Booker kissed him on the forehead. Booker's beard touched the two-day growth of the other man. When he stepped back, his friend turned away as the tears rolled down his cheeks. Bessie, weeping herself, produced a wet cloth to help restore her husband's composure.

"What about a shave?" Booker proposed.

"Me or you?" Sid asked with obvious pleasure.

"We can't get any service," Bessie explained. "We're paying for a private room, but we have to hire a private duty nurse to make sure he's watched overnight. I can't be here all the time."

"I understand," Booker said to console. "Maybe I can fill in so that you can get some rest."

"The boys have been wonderful, but they have to keep the business going. They visit every night, and they come whenever I need them." Bessie referred to her two sons who were in their father's appraisal firm.

Before lunch arrived, Booker used Sid's shaving kit to give the patient a safety razor shave. He worked slowly and gently, and finished the job with a hair combing and a pat of aftershave lotion on the pale gray cheeks. Sid kept his eyes closed, but responded as Booker moved his chin to use the razor. Bessie watched in amazement.

"You are the last person I ever expected to do something like this," she said as she stood behind Booker and admired the relaxed face of her husband.

"Why so?" Booker asked.

"You have been so rigid, so formal. A great friend. Don't get me wrong. We love to have fun with you and Ellen, but I never counted on you in our personal lives. I never imagined that you could be so tender, so sensitive."

"I never imagined either," Booker as Winn admitted. "Why don't you take a break and let me try to get Sid to eat something."

The early morning radiation treatment had not only killed cancer cells, but it had also killed Sid's appetite. He could not tolerate anything offered to him. He did take a few ounces of fortified milk drink through a flexible straw, but it was only a gesture to acknowledge Booker's effort. He reached for Booker's hand when the food tray was removed.

"Don't go yet, will you?"

"I'm not going anywhere," Booker assured him. "You don't have to talk. Just rest."

Sid slept most of the afternoon between inspections by nurses and a visit by a consulting physician who examined Sid for suspected pneumonia. Later, suction equipment was brought into the room and a tube put into Sid's mouth. Another medication was added to his IV drip.

The news for Bessie as night fell was not good. The oncologist was suspending the radiation treatments. Sid was sinking from fluid in his lungs. His cancer-ravaged body could not defend itself. Pneumonia was a common cause of death in these cases. It was just a matter of days or even hours. And although Bessie had expected the worst, the actual words struck her like a physical blow. Fortunately, her sons were on hand to support her. Booker drifted away to give them the intimate space that they needed, ate supper in the hospital cafeteria, and took a cab the few miles back to Little Neck Road.

Buffy greeted him. "Mother called to let me know you were at the hospital. Mrs. Taylor talked to her. It's bad, isn't it?"

"Sid may not last the week," Booker said simply. "I'll be at the hospital in the late morning. Don't worry about me."

The next morning Booker fixed himself breakfast, reported to work at five, unloaded trucks until eight, and then took a cab to the hospital.

Sid Taylor was six years older than Booker. Still, at sixty, very few anglos considered it a good age to die. Sid had feared and resented his disease to the point of bitterness. Then he wished to die in combat against it as if to say, "Kill me, you bastard." The wish carried the hope of delivering himself and his emotionally tormented wife and family from further pain.

There were few opportunities for Booker and Sid to be alone, and when they were, Sid was capable of only a few coherent words. No one knew the clarity of his thoughts. If Booker had one prayer for his brother, it was that the man find resolution and peace before the body expired. He held this prayer as his focus in every conscious moment, whether it be unloading trucks or waiting outside Sid's room while the doctors examined him on their morning rounds.

Booker moved the untouched breakfast tray and set up the bedside table for shaving.

"Did I dream that you shaved me?" Sid asked weakly as Booker put the lather on his face.

"No, you didn't dream it," Booker said with a smile.

"I want to die," Sid said.

"I know," Booker acknowledged.

"I'm not afraid."

"There is nothing to fear."

"I want to go home," Sid insisted.

In previous days, Sid had attempted to threaten and implore his wife and sons into taking him home to die in his own bed. Their reasons why this request could not be honored never satisfied him. But the home to which he now referred was of another plane, and Booker knew it.

"You can go home," Booker assured him.

That night, with Bessie taken home in exhaustion and the older son out of the room, Sid had another lucid moment. He recognized Booker at his bedside and gave him the gift for which he had prayed.

"It's beautiful," Sid reported with awe in his voice. "I can see it. It's beautiful."

The next day, Booker shaved Sid in the morning, but the patient was too weak to cooperate with voluntary head movements although he was conscious of the process and said Winn's name. In the late afternoon, with Bessie and both sons in the room, Sid seemed to hallucinate. The words "home" and "beautiful" could be distinguished. Booker explained to them the meaning.

"He is ready. He is at peace. All he needs is for you to release him."

They understood, and one by one they went to the head of the bed and whispered their goodbyes. Sid expired less than an hour later, his face serene, almost smiling.

The funeral was Saturday. Ellen attended, but Booker would not go. The last day of September was mild and sunny. Booker worked his three hours at the loading dock and then took a cab to the oceanfront. He accessed the beach through the small Norwegian Lady park and turned north toward the residential oceanfront. Other people were walking near the tide line as the frothy surf ebbed and flowed. The white seagulls and a few brown pelicans were active. A man threw a stick repeatedly beyond the surf to the inexhaustible enthusiasm of a black Labrador Retriever. Off shore, late-starting sport fishing boats were running hard to the site of hovering gulls, hoping to find a frenzy of bluefish feeding on their fall migration up the coast.

Sitting in the sand, watching the boats head for the blues was an appropriate ritual to honor a man who loved to fish. For Booker, Sid would always be on his flybridge headed out to the Gulf Stream or, better, on the back of a great marlin forever frolicking in the sea.

CHAPTER TWENTY

In their discussions about Booker as Winn, the Conovers agreed that he was too calm, too relaxed. The missing facial mannerisms bothered them, too. They did not consider that the mannerisms disappeared with the uncertain thoughts which had produced them. The cause for the change had to be drugs or mental imbalance.

"He seems content to take whatever chance might bring," Buffy observed.

"He isolates himself and is secretive," Ellen complained in recalling his refusal to attend Sid's funeral.

"He doesn't talk unless you ask him a question," Theo said. "And where does he walk for three hours in the morning?"

On Tuesday afternoon, Theo picked his father up at Buffy's and took him to his psychiatric appointment, and then to the family internist for a complete physical, including a hopefully revealing blood test.

The psychiatrist reported that he could make no immediate diagnosis and required further sessions to explore Winn's explanation for his bizarre manner of leaving home.

The internist reported that Winn was in excellent health, with the best blood pressure and cholesterol he had had in ten years. There was no evidence of substance abuse of any kind. The doctor congratulated Winn on his weight loss and concomitant gain in muscle mass.

The Conovers, wanting an easy answer to their dilemma, were ambivalent about the results.

"Maybe it's just a spiritual thing," Buffy suggested. "Bill took a comparative religion course at William and Mary and said that in India, religious Hindus live part of their lives as householders, and then they leave their families in old age to become monks."

"Yeah," Theo said as a dismissal. "Dad, the monk. That's real consistent with selling real estate for thirty years. Real probable for a man who stopped going to church when I was in high school. Dad is no saint."

"He is if you ask Bessie Taylor," their mother said. "Sid's boys sent flowers to the house. They were for your father! I am so confused."

"So he was there for them when their father died," Theo countered. "They are grateful. What's the big deal?"

"It's a big deal to them," Ellen corrected. "Sid was angry and resentful when your father arrived. He died in peace. They believe your father had a lot to do with it."

"OK," Theo said to appease his mother.

"Why don't you invite Dad back into the house," Buffy suggested.

"What would I say to him? What would we do? He's so different, it scares me. He won't watch television. He won't come to the office. It would be like living with a stranger."

"Mom's got a point," Theo said.

"Well, go to dinner together. Do something!" Buffy was emphatic.

"George Pappas has invited your father to play golf this weekend. He has known us for a long time. I want to hear what he thinks before I do anything," Ellen said.

George Pappas was a well-known Virginia Beach restaurateur. His oceanfront steak house was a landmark. But his reputation was made not as a congenial host, but as a political mover and shaker. When the Democratic Party machine in Virginia folded to party liberals with the nomination of George McGovern for President, George Pappas, then President of the Virginia Beach Chamber of Commerce, was in position to move into the power void. Rather than run for office himself, Pappas became a major fund-raiser for local and state candidates. His stocky figure and bulging eyes became a fixture at backroom political sessions where his support dictated political careers. As President of the State Restaurant Association, he was a leader in successful liquor-by-the-drink referendums. And when Virginia turned Republican, George Pappas was again on the right side with his money and his influence.

Winn Conover had been the man Pappas trusted with the buying and selling of his commercial real estate. Conover Real Estate had made substantial profits for Pappas over the years. The older man considered Winn and Ellen among his few friends. He had plenty of political enemies.

George came for Booker shortly after 2 P.M., late, as was his habit, for a 2:30 tee time at the Princess Anne Country Club members-only golf course. Neither man had improved his game in ten or more years of playing together and had, in fact, lost strokes on their handicaps as they had gained middle-age weight.

George had been prepared by Ellen for the change in Winn's appearance. His intent was to pretend that nothing had changed since their last game together, to avoid any mention of Winn's disappearance. When he picked up Winn's golf bag at the real estate office, Ellen made George take Winn's golf shoes and a coordinated set of golfing attire. "All he's got are blue jeans and a baggy old suit. He can't play at the club in those," she warned.

Ellen was right. When Booker came out of Buffy's house to greet his bronzed and expensively attired friend, he looked more like a grounds keeper than a country club member. The blue suit, the shoes, and the checkered shirt were not Winn's normal fashion statement. George mentally crossed off clothes, a subject they had often talked about, from his safe list of conversation topics.

The greeting was sincere, nevertheless, and the two men were soon headed for the club in George's Lincoln Towncar.

"We'll play the front nine and see how we feel,"

George said. "If your handicap dropped with your waistline, I'm in trouble."

George was referring to their standard of ten dollars a hole for match play. It was small stakes to men of their means, but important in the way men compete with each other. To win $40 or $50 over eighteen holes would give one bragging rights over the other for months. Many times they had challenged each other over eighteen holes only to come out even.

"You want to hit a bucket of balls at the driving range before we start?" George asked.

"What about our tee time?" Booker asked out of consideration.

"Let the suckers wait."

"No, let's go ahead and play. It's a beautiful day. I wish we could walk the course instead of using the carts."

"No way," George retorted. "It's still against club rules. It slows up the play too much."

"But the course is so inviting." Booker saw into Winn's memory. "Golf used to be a pastoral exercise."

"It's a damned expensive walk in the country," George observed. "Too costly to dilly dally. We've got to push the members through to keep pace with the budget. Do you think people will pay the initiation fee to join the club if they can't get a tee time?"

"It seems like we painted ourselves into a box," Booker observed.

"Who's got time to walk a round of golf and admire the azaleas? Those days are gone forever," George argued. "If you have enough money to join this club, most of us have to keep hustling to stay here."

"That hasn't been true for you for more than ten years," Booker as Winn recalled.

"Do you remember when I was the first Greek admitted to the club? If I hadn't owned half of the board members, I never would have gotten in."

"Was it so important?"

"You're damn right it was important. Greeks were just behind Jews and Blacks on their don't-come line. Sure, they would take your money and your votes, but don't ever think about joining their club."

"And now that you are in their club, are you at peace?"

"Hell, no."

"Then what is the purpose?"

"To show them that I am as good as they are."

"But they are prejudiced and unkind. Why do you want to be like them?"

"I don't know," George said in exasperation. "Aren't you one of them?"

"Yes," Booker said, "but I can change. I can choose to include rather than to exclude."

"I joined the enemy, and now the enemy is me," George concluded. "Is that it?"

"There is no enemy," Booker said.

The valet attendant was at the driver's door, so the men got out and watched their golf bags being taken from the car trunk and placed on the rear deck of the electric cart. Then they went into the clubhouse with Winn's golf attire, and he changed clothes in the locker room.

George hit first, a muscular drive with a slight hook that carried the ball into the playable rough. He was pleased. Booker had a more relaxed shot that did not carry as far as George's, but was near center on the fairway.

Booker's third shot on the par four first hole landed in a deep sand trap to the right of the pin. George was on the green, but a long way from the hole.

Exiting the golf cart and seeing the position of Booker's ball, George could not suppress his pleasure. "You are going to need a Kempsville to get out of this."

Kempsville referred to a match game played years earlier at the Kempsville Manor Golf Club. Winn lay two in a huge sand bunker that was so deep the flag could not be seen. The par five was the longest hole on the course. It had taken George five to get on the green. He would ultimately take a two-putt seven.

George had insisted on rules as Winn addressed the ball with his sand wedge.

"Don't touch the sand before you hit the ball," were his last words as he went out of sight onto the green above. He was sure of winning the hole.

Winn struck the ball, and it popped over the burly bunker in a spray of sand. The next thing he heard was George screaming. The ball had cleared the lip of the bunker and rolled downhill directly into the cup for an eagle-three. George ran to the edge of the sandtrap. "You threw it up! You had to throw it, and the damn thing went in!"

It was only after George examined the imprint of Winn's stroke in the sand pit was he convinced that the shot had been legitimate. Without doubt, it was the greatest single golf shot of Winn's life. It was a memory that the two men enjoyed sharing. It was ultimately their reason for playing the game. The possibility for greatness, for remarkable luck, always existed even among duffers.

Booker took two swipes at the ball to clear the trap and three more strokes to put it in the hole. Winn Conover would have cursed his sand wedge and his putter for the terrible eight, but Booker was unperturbed.

"One up," George reminded his companion, but he wished that Winn had demonstrated more anguish in the loss. Winn had always been good for that. When you beat him, he suffered in the extreme. Without it, what was the fun of winning?

George won the second hole by two strokes as Booker's five iron approach shot went into the trees. To George's consternation, the loser seemed to enjoy the hole.

On three, Booker rolled in a long putt to half the hole after George had made his bogey. Normally, Winn would have danced in mockery after denying George the win. Booker seemed unaware of the score. George did not appreciate the tactic.

"Stop daydreaming," George said to Booker as they approached the fourth tee. "You are down two. Take the honors."

Booker's tee shot went into the water. He teed up again and his second shot went into the water. As he rummaged in the pockets of his golf bag for a third ball, George was uncontrollably glib.

"You have to pay for any fish you kill."

"I'll try to be more careful," Booker said, recognizing the humor and enjoying it.

Booker's third shot cleared the small lake and landed in good position on the green. George's first tee shot hit the rim of the embankment fronting the green and bounced back into the lake. He was incredulous.

"It could have bounced the other way, and I'd have a birdie," he shouted. "It's not fair."

His second shot sliced to a far extent of the lake and splashed. George was furious and pounded his driver into the ground as if to bend the shaft. A string of profanities carried over the water and seemed magnified. When he calmed down, he selected another club and remarked to Booker, "I had you. All I had to do was put the ball on the green."

"It's just a game," Booker said simply.

"The hell it is," George decried. And then he hit his third shot in the water and ruefully conceded the hole.

At the end of eight holes, they were even. George was disappointed with his play and complained that he was off his game. At nine, he missed his final putt and Booker holed out to go one up for the match.

"I should have beaten you," George complained.

"Why?" Booker asked.

"Because I wanted it more than you did," George asserted.

"When is desire the criteria? It seems to lead to disappointment," Booker responded.

"You don't play with the same fire," George accused to avoid the question.

"Who needs fire on a day like today?" Booker said with a gesture to the landscape. "The grass doesn't keep score."

"You are starting to talk like that guy on Kung Fu who plays the Chinese monk," George complained.

"Is that so?" Booker asked.

"Let's hit the bar," George said to end the conversation. "I'm finished for the day. I hate golf. I don't know why I bother to play."

When George reported to Ellen, he had mixed emotions concerning his afternoon with Booker as Winn. "He's quiet, less excitable. I hit three tee shots into the lake, and he didn't even taunt me. He won the match, but you couldn't tell from hole to hole if he won or lost. It was like he was out for a walk in the woods. At first I didn't think I had a good time. I swore that I was never going to play golf with Winn again. But now that I think it over, we had our moments. I could have been less tense and enjoyed it more. It wasn't Winn's fault. He seemed to have a great time. He doesn't drink anymore. Did you know that? I have never been with Winn at the club that he didn't have a couple of drinks, but not this time. I drank anyway. He didn't seem to mind. He's different. I'll have to give you that. But is he crazy? I don't think so. But he is definitely out of the fast lane. That's for sure. He's lost his edge. The way he is right now, he's perfectly worthless for business or politics. Ellen, you do what you have to do. It's the old story of the horse that won't run or the dog that won't hunt. If you don't want a pet, you have to make hard decisions."

CHAPTER TWENTY-ONE

"Mr. Conover?" the young woman with the baby in the grocery cart asked with some alarm. "Is that you?"

"Hello, Libby," Booker responded as he looked up from bagging her purchases. "Sorry I didn't notice you. What a beautiful baby."

The attention to her baby, which normally would have set off prideful display posturing, was ignored as the woman froze in shock.

"You disappeared. Everybody is looking for you."

"Not anymore," Booker assured her.

The older woman at the register who knew the substitute early morning bag boy as Booker Jones, had stopped processing items over the scanner and was staring too.

"It's OK," Booker said to the cashier. "In my former life I was known as Mr. Conover. Libby was a bridesmaid in my daughter's wedding."

Neither of the women seemed satisfied.

"Does Buffy know?" Libby asked.

"I'm not sure she knows about my job. I'm staying with Bill and Buffy, but they are so busy we really don't get to communicate."

"I don't see much of her either since the baby was born," Libby said, still tense.

"What's the baby's name?" Booker said as he stepped closer to view the child.

"Her name is Erica Ann. She's eight months old tomorrow. What is your name now?" Libby asked cautiously.

"These folks know me as Booker Jones," the bagger said without hesitation.

Libby just nodded and forced up a twisted smile. She didn't know what more to say, although her mind was racing with questions. She desperately wanted to get to a telephone.

Booker insisted on helping the young mother to her car with the groceries. There were few customers, as it was only nine o'clock. Libby was confused by Mr. Conover's naturalness. He should have been mortified, in her opinion. Buffy's father working as a supermarket bag boy under an assumed name had to be the most exciting scandal of Libby's life. She relished the idea that she might be the first person to expose him.

Back at the check-out lane, the cashier could not contain her curiosity.

"So you have two names?" she asked.

"Actually," Booker responded, "I have three names. My third name might be difficult for you to pronounce. It is only used by members of my Indian clan."

"Oh," the woman said, forgetting to close her mouth. In some situations, it is best not to probe people you don't know, especially when you start to encounter weirdness. The cashier thought that this was one of those situations. "You want to check the bag inventory?" she suggested. "We use a lot more plastic than we do paper."

Buffy did not reach her father on the phone until after four o'clock, although she had started calling before noon. Booker had not heard the signal earlier because he had been mowing Buffy's lawn. Later, while weeding and winterizing the plants along her back fence with pine straw, he had lain down on the grass and taken a nap in the bright afternoon sun.

After Buffy accepted her father's explanation as to why he had not answered the phone, she gave him the reason for her urgency. "Did you see Libby Stormont this morning?"

"Yes, I did. She has a beautiful daughter named Erica Ann."

"Dad, are you working as a bag boy at Winn-Dixie?"

"Just in the early mornings as a substitute when the regular employees don't show," he explained.

"My God, Dad. You don't have to do that."

"I'm doing it as a favor to Wilson James, the night manager," Booker said.

"Who is Wilson James to us?" Buffy continued to probe.

"He's the good man who hired me to unload the trucks."

"What trucks?" Buffy almost shouted in reflex.

"The trucks that come in from five to eight. They have a problem getting people to come in that early."

"You are unloading trucks . . ." Buffy's voice trailed off in exasperation. "That's what you are doing at sunrise? We thought that you were out every morning to commune with nature."

"I do," her father said. "You can see the sun come up perfectly from the loading dock." The words might have been facetious, but Booker intended them only as descriptive.

"Libby said that you were using another name."

"That's right."

"What's the name?"

"The entire name is Booker Washington Jones."

"Daddy, that's a black man's name."

"I know. A black man gave it to me."

"Daddy, I am so damned confused, my head is spinning."

"It's simple, really. I needed a new identification, and the first person I met after I left home gave it to me. He happened to be black."

"OK, but why are you working? You've got a ton of money in the bank. And why as a bag boy? It's demeaning."

"Demeaning to whom?" Booker asked gently.

"Demeaning to me, to the whole family. How do you think I felt when Libby called to tell me that you bagged her groceries?"

"How do you feel now?"

"I don't know. Why are you doing it?"

"Helpful deeds are our natural duty," he said. "It was work that presented itself."

"I can't stand it when you talk like that," Buffy said, near tears.

"Talk like what?" Booker asked sincerely.

"Like you are some kind of guru!" Buffy accused.

"Forgive me, Honey. I certainly don't intend to sound that way."

"Well, you do. And it scares me."

"Why is that?"

"Because it's not the Daddy I remember."

"That Daddy never had time for you," he reminded her. "This Daddy has all the time there ever was or ever will be for you."

There was a long silence on the other end of the line. He could hear her attempting to control her tears. "Well, I guess there are some compensations," she said, trying to cope by humor. "You never cut my grass before."

"Come home, and we'll cook out tonight," Booker suggested.

"Bill might have to work late," Buffy said sadly.

"Call him, Honey. Remind him that you love him and that your career and his are always second to your relationship. Use your charms. Get the man home tonight."

"We'll grill some bluefish filets," Buffy said. "Anything special you want?"

"Pick up some ears of Silver Queen corn, and I will show you how to roast them Indian style," Booker said with enthusiasm.

"That sounds great," she said. "I've got to go. My staff is wondering what's wrong with me."

"There is nothing wrong with you, darling girl," Booker said.

"You're right, Dad. See you about quarter to six."

The next day, Booker kept Winn's third appointment with the psychiatrist. The doctor had been advised of his patient's unusual employment earlier in the day. Because of the community status of the patient and the high profile of the case, the doctor was willing to make personal reports to the Conover family.

"We can continue with the sessions if you insist," he told Ellen, "but your husband appears to be centered and well-oriented. If he seems strange, it is because he outpictures an idealized world in which he views all people as interconnected. It's a spiritual premise that many religions subscribe to, but few individuals actualize. We see obsessive cases in our practice and some religiously delusioned patients, but your husband is not one of them. Frankly, he is very refreshing. Very natural. Confident, yet humble. I've taken recent seminars from new age psychoanalysts whom I found less convincing than your husband.

"He has undergone a transformation of character which is obviously evident in his personality and behavior. To you, and even to himself, he is a different person. I can appreciate how disturbing this is to you and your family, but, although it is rare, it is not clinically abnormal. People change. Sometimes they change radically. Some change for the good, some for the bad. A successful leader in real estate chooses to unload trucks. It happens.

"A colleague of mine in North Carolina had a similar case. A man who headed a computer empire took a trip to West Virginia and observed people living in poverty. It affected him so profoundly that he wanted to leave his business and move to West Virginia to start a private anti-poverty program. His stockholders forced him into therapy. In the end, the therapist had to tell them that their profit generator had rationally altered the purpose of his life. The patient was not deranged, he was just compassionate and unselfish in ways they could not understand. Finally, they had no choice. They had to let him go.

"You say that you have little in common with your husband as he is today. You ask me if he will return to his old self. I can't say. But if I were in your place, I would not count on it. When he tells me that he cannot return to his former materialistic lifestyle, I believe him.

"Let me ask you this. If your sister decided tomorrow to become a nun and entered a convent, would she cease to be your sister? If your son became a priest, would he cease to be your son? Yes, I understand that marriage is different. So the ball is really in your court, isn't it? If your husband has chosen a contemplative lifestyle, can you live with it? That's the question, isn't it?"

CHAPTER TWENTY-TWO

"I can arrange it," Wilson James said in response to Booker's request. "A hundred pounds is about $40. They can pick it up at the nearest Norfolk store. What's the Catholic Worker going to do with a hundred pounds of instant grits a week?"

"You are kidding me," James said to Booker's explanation. "I didn't know anything like that was going on. I mean, we donate a few turkeys and hams for Thanksgiving and Christmas, but six days a week to all comers is an entirely different thing. You sure you don't want to put your name on it? Forty bucks must be a lot of money to you."

Ellen had avoided direct contact with her estranged husband as a defense from her own emotions, but with the medical reports in, she had to face her real fears. Although she was still angry by Winn's disappearance as a thoughtless act of rejection aimed at her, the evidence was mounting that the wrong had not been premeditated nor the intent malicious. Winn was contrite enough, but his personality was so restrained. She almost wished that he would come home in a rage, kick the dogs off the bed, and demand sex.

At least he could come back to the office and take charge of the politics and the ole boy network that was still important to business. Theo could sell property by hustle and persistence, but his father could accomplish more on the golf course in one afternoon than Theo could in a month. Winn's Kiwanis Club, his UVA Alumni Association, and his personal alignment with the political personalities in power provided profitable contacts that Theo might never be able to earn. Ellen would be permitted to work with wives of the big shots in finding a new house, but she knew that her generation was not going to overcome the gender gap when it came to deal-making. Tidewater men had a private power club to which she could never belong.

There were, however, compensations. When Ellen and her peers relaxed around the country club pool and enjoyed their gossip, their husbands were still stressfully competing with each other on the golf course or in the card room. They never relented from their goal of winning. Every act of life was a race of some kind, and the intensity of it would kill them and leave their widows with ten or more years of life in which to spend their accumulated wealth. It was a common topic of conversation among the older women around the pool as the tanned, handsome cabana boys brought them their lunch and cocktails. It was a fantasy conversation: what would you do if your husband died tomorrow? The most frequent first impressions had to do with exotic travel involving one or more of the cabana boys. It was play, but it was play that brought up eventualities. And amid the laughter, vulnerabilities emerged. Few women were prepared to replace their husbands. It was too impractical.

One subject in the what-if game was taboo. The women never played what-if-your-husband-leaves-you. It was the ultimate terror of their socioeconomic age group.

Ellen had depended on Winn to initiate most of the important events in their married life. Now, with him acting like a conscientious objector to normal affairs, she telephoned him to propose dinner together. He was warm and enthusiastic, and offered to introduce her to New Mexican cuisine at a restaurant he discovered in Virginia Beach.

The evening began on the left foot as Ellen called for Booker as Winn in her Cadillac entirely overdressed for the Blue Corn Cafe. The restaurant, although charming in southwestern decor, was unpretentious and located in a second-class, outdated strip shopping center. The food, however, proved to be authentic and reasonably priced. Ellen's anticipation had been more trendy and upscale.

The situation was strangely formal for Ellen. She felt like she was on a blind date. She had not accustomed herself to Winn's white hair and beard nor to his trim figure. Every year of their marriage since their weight gain, they had promised to diet together and use their health club memberships more often. Now Winn had achieved the goal and she had not. The comparison made her ever more self-conscious than she already was.

Booker was a generous host, explaining the items

on the menu and making recommendations. Ellen ordered a frozen Margarita. Booker was pleased to find hot Indian tea available although it was not on the menu.

"Don't you want a cocktail?" Ellen asked.

"No, thanks. The tea is fine."

"Have you stopped drinking alcohol?" Ellen asked pointedly.

"I don't know," Booker answered honestly. "I haven't had the desire for it the last few times it was offered, but I can't say I wouldn't take a drink."

"It's never been a problem for you," she observed. "You've been too high to drive home from parties, but you weren't a drunk. A couple of drinks a day is good for your heart. That's what the doctors are saying."

Ellen asked Booker to order, so he had carne adovada, tender pork cooked in red chile, chile rellenos, the green chilies stuffed with cheese and batter fried, posole, the hominy that replaces Spanish rice on New Mexican tables, blue corn tortillas and pinto beans brought to the table. The owner-chef brought the food out personally. He wanted to see who had ordered the traditional supper so far away from its source. The Hispanic man seemed to take an immediate liking to her husband. Booker amazed her by speaking a little Spanish. The Santa Fe connection that seemed to bond the strangers, however, was a nuisance to Ellen.

To top it off, Ellen did not like the food, although Booker assured her it was excellent. The main dishes seemed to Ellen to be peasant cooking which relied too heavily on chile sauces that were too hot for her tastes. She saw no sophistication or value either in the beans, the tortillas, or the hominy. She ate what she could to appease Booker, who was enjoying the meal. Meanwhile, she consumed three large Margaritas.

In place of dessert, each ordered coffee so that they could linger over the table. Ellen had issues that she wanted addressed.

"Do you love me?"

Booker was not chagrined by Ellen's directness. "Of course, I love you."

"Then why won't you act normal and help me in the business?" she asked almost as a plea.

"There was a time in my life to strive for wealth and power, but that time has passed. I cannot return to it. It is a whirlwind that might snatch me away from my contentment." Booker spoke slowly, allowing the words to flow without effort or precognition.

"How can you be content to unload trucks and bag groceries? You are only ten years from retirement." Ellen was referring to Winn's age, wondering how long he could endure a regime of manual labor.

"We could retire now," Booker as Winn suggested.

"I can't retire," Ellen retorted. "What would I do? I'm too young to drop out. My whole life revolves around real estate. I enjoy it. I enjoy the social contacts. I enjoy being the boss. It is who I am. I can't quit now."

"I understand," Booker said in the same unruffled tone.

"So where does that leave us?" Ellen asked. "Do you expect me to go to work every day to support you? Do you expect me to go to the parties, and the conventions, and the charity events alone? And how do I explain the absence of my husband? Do I tell them that you have lost interest in everything that they feel is important? How am I supposed to handle it?"

"It may be difficult for you," Booker agreed.

"What is it that you want?" Ellen demanded. "What do you expect?"

"I have no expectations," Booker replied.

"Do you want a divorce?" Ellen asked in dismay.

"That is for you to say. I don't want to be in conflict with you."

"Well, you are in conflict with me whether you want it or not. Do you understand what a divorce means? Would I lose the house? Would we have to sell the business to divide the assets? You are very threatening to me."

"Please, please," Booker said to console her. "You will lose nothing. I want nothing. Be at peace about your home and your business."

"You say that now, but when the attorneys get hold of you and see what we are worth, they will make you fight for your share."

"I seek no attorney," Booker said. "Bring whatever documents are required to satisfy you about your security, and I will sign them."

"Are you serious?" she asked, gaining some control over her emotions.

"I want you to be happy," Booker assured her.

"Happiness is not dependent on possessions. I gladly give them to you."

"The doctors say that you are not crazy, but no sane person gives up what he has spent a lifetime building."

"People do it every day," Booker said.

"What people?" Ellen demanded.

"The ones who die," Booker said with a humorous smile.

"That's maudlin," Ellen was not satisfied. "Are you planning on dying soon?"

"I tried to explain that to you when I returned from Santa Fe. From one perspective, the person that you knew already died. It was the metaphysical death of a false reality. The man you see before you emerged from that process. I wish that you could join me in this new world."

"I can't." Ellen was emphatic. "It is too uncertain for me. You are too uncertain for me. I want the old Winn back. You are like his zombie. Look at you. Your marriage of twenty-seven years is falling apart and you act like it means nothing. Get angry! Cry! Do something!"

Booker saw the deep hurt in Ellen's eyes and his empathy for her did produce tears. They sat in silence, their cheeks wet, as Booker poured out his healing love. But the warmth he generated could not penetrate the barrier she raised around her own spiritual heart. She would not be consoled. Her position would not be moved. She fed on her pain as confirmation of a vengeful God who punished and destroyed. The problem with Winn seemed to confirm her darkest suspicions: life was an intolerable mess that could be endured only by taking all the pleasures that money could buy. There was no real security. There was no enduring happiness. Every seeming happiness was merely situational. And this situation, she concluded, was terrible, but survivable.

Ellen allowed her husband to kiss her goodbye when she took him back to Little Neck. On the drive to Norfolk, Ellen felt relieved that the inevitable subject of divorce had been faced. Tomorrow she would call her attorney. Tomorrow she would face the children. It would be another terrible night alone. Thank God for her dogs. At least they remained constant until death. She decided to go on a diet, to take a cruise with one of her divorced girlfriends. Perhaps she would meet a nice man. Maybe she would have an affair with one of the stewards. If Winn left her most of the money, she could do anything she wanted. Somehow the prospect did not elevate her mood. She went to bed dejected, wondering what she had done to deserve her humiliating fate.

CHAPTER TWENTY-THREE

The car stereo seemed to be on whenever Booker rode with Buffy or Theo. It was a habit like turning on a television set as soon as they came into the house. Conversations had to be conducted around the programming in competition with it. There was an unconscious rudeness about the habit that seemed to say that the human companions in the space were somehow less important than the technical ones.

Booker could retire to his bedroom when the television preempted human contact, but riding in the car he was subjected to whatever was playing. Much of the popular music included saccharin love songs in adoration of a romantic other. Booker first heard the songs as an outcry for love. Then he found that he could turn much of the music and its lyrics into hymns of praise if The Great Spirit were the object of the song instead of the human lover. With this insight, he listened carefully to the ballad lyrics, made the mental substitution, and enjoyed the music as much as his youthful companions. The pop love songs became holy songs of worship when the object of the romance was God.

"I didn't know you like my music," Buffy said in amazement. Her father was singing along with the CD that she was playing.

"That's one of my current favorites," he admitted, and they both joined in on the chorus.

In contrast, Theo perceived his father's enjoyment of contemporary music as another perverse manifestation of his change. Formerly, his father would have demanded that the offensive music be turned off. Now Theo turned the music off to avoid his father's singing. He could not stand ludicrous behavior in the man who had always required decorum from him. He saw no humor or irony in the role reversal.

Booker as Winn had reached détente with his daughter and was in the process of gaining her trust again. The more difficult resolution with Ellen seemed possible, although Booker did not consider the conditions her emotional closure might require. Theo presented the most disturbing barriers to reconciliation. Why was the history of fathers and sons so confrontational? Why must they be antagonistic in the space between their maturing generations? Booker searched for peace with his son that was beyond strategy.

In the world, a father hopes to hand over his property and his pedantry in a neat pedagogical package. In this manner he passes his pedigree and his prejudices to his progeny and satisfies himself on the progression of life. In practice, the proof is seldom a facsimile of the engraving. Like father, like son is a distortion. For each, the mirror is a daily reminder of the genetic diatribe.

Booker realized that he could not relate to Theo in an anthropocentric way. And yet he felt an obligation to share the nature of his transformation with his son. It would not be an attempt to justify his new life by seeking his son's understanding or approval. He rather wanted to save his son from the needless burdens he bore; burdens that Winn Conover had helped to strap into place, as if preparing his son to climb a mountain. Booker wanted the boy to know that there were no mountains to climb. The struggle was an illusion.

This was the gift Booker wanted to give. If his father had given it to him, how different his life might have been. But recalling his own emergence into manhood, would he have heard his father's wisdom? Booker turned the pages in the library of Winn's memory and did not find a young man who might stop in his pursuit of self-worth to find the real Self. No voice, especially a father's, would be heard. If time had been a governing factor in the truth of Reality, Booker could have regretted Winn's life. But since he knew that the path did not depend on a temporal dimension, he let go of that judgment. He knew, too, that he must let go his attachment to Theo. It was difficult. Every time he saw Theo, it was like looking at himself.

The opportunity to talk privately with Theo came mid week after Booker's date with Ellen at the Blue Corn Cafe. Theo needed his father's signature on the title of the Ford Explorer to effect the transfer of ownership.

By the middle of October, the resort side of Virginia Beach reverts from heavy tourist traffic to local beachcombers. Even the hardy Canadians who favor the shoulder season hotel rates and will swim in ice water have abandoned the beaches and the public golf courses. Along Atlantic and Pacific Avenues, which parallel the oceanfront, shops and restaurants have closed for the season. Storm fronts carrying the potential of hurricanes haunt the shoreline, and formations of geese can be seen headed for the wetlands of the Great Dismal Swamp.

Theo was sensing the autumn of the commercial real estate market at the Beach, too. It was too early to anticipate what major resort properties might be up for sale. Those decisions were being made by accountants and attorneys. Theo wished that he was privy to their discussions so that he might recommend sale options and thus obtain the listings. A big motel sale in March or April was the cream on any Beach realtor's cappuccino.

Theo had enjoyed the cream of his father's listings when he had joined the firm in May. The properties sold, and his income soared. The business carried him through the summer and into the fall, but now he had no properties of his own to show. He had no deals in the works. During the publicity of his father's disappearance and for weeks after, the leaving of his name with secretaries of important prospects brought a return call. Business associates of his father were anxious for details of the case, and were willing to help Theo salvage what Winn had initiated. New initiatives, however, were

not so welcomed. Theo could not command the respect accorded his father, and more and more his
telephone messages were ignored. Important people
were also unavailable to go to lunch with a surro-
gate. By October, Theo had the clothes and the car
to make a successful appearance, but he had no sig-
nificant appointments. He was existing on split com-
missions earned by showing walk-in prospects other
realtors' low-end listings. It was the equivalent of
selling used cars. As much as he hated to do it, he
was going to have to ask for his father's advice.

The two men sat in Buffy's family room at the
rear of the house. The jalousied windows afforded
a wide angle view of the wooded yard where
Booker had raked neat piles of leaves and pine
straw. The cold rain driven from the northeast made
the day seem damp and dreary. Booker had a small
fire crackling in the red brick fireplace to take the
chill off the long rectangular room that had once
been a porch. After the title document was signed,
Booker offered Theo Indian herbal tea and sweet
frybread that he had made and flavored with cinna-
mon and honey. They sat facing each other in a
comfortable grouping of easy chairs and lamp tables
on either side of the hearth.

Theo thought that he had never seen his father
so relaxed, so domesticated as to serve tea and
some treat he had made himself. The quiet seemed
odd, too. No television. No radio. The rain beat
against the windows in gusts of wind, and the fire
made soft popping sounds, but Theo could still hear
himself breathing.

Booker, in the Pueblo Indian way, did not rush into conversation. He sat content, listening to the wind and the fire until Theo spoke.

"Dad, what did you do to generate your listings? The well seems to have run dry for me."

"Like all of life, career is based on relationship," Booker began. "Trust. Faith. Confidence. These qualities must be nurtured. Show yourself among the people you would seek to serve. Be open. Take responsibility for your thoughts. There will be many opportunities to serve." Booker's metaphor was almost lost on Theo, although it was delivered in a deliberate tone.

"Fine," Theo lamented. "Dad, I need help here, not philosophical mumbo jumbo. Are you saying join some clubs where I can develop prospects?"

"That's one way of looking at it," Booker said. "If you need a new suit, you won't find it by hanging around a candy store."

"OK, I get that," Theo said. "So what clubs are the best? Sales and Marketing Execs? Young Republicans? Kiwanis Club? I need to get something going fast."

"Character is not established in haste. A selfish motive, however, will be quickly found out. Offer yourself as a servant who is willing to do the most menial job. Do each job well. Do it cheerfully. Small responsibilities lead to greater ones. Respect is earned by performance, not by rank. Those who you support will support you."

"That could take years," Theo complained. "I need action now."

"I am with you," Booker acknowledged. "First, understand what it means to act now. Taking responsibility for your thoughts is the act of now. Each person believes that he is special, and from this specialness we distort everything around us to support the idea of individuality. It makes living very complex. The truth is simple, clear, and direct if you can suspend your specialness and be open to it. That is how you live now. Now is the only place you can live. Now is the only time you can act." Booker wanted passionately for Theo to have his experience.

"I know that you are trying to help me. I can see that you are sincere, but I don't know what the hell you are talking about! Things might be simple for you, Dad, but they are damn confusing to me. You are saying be a stand-up guy with character and service to humanity, and that's fine as far as it goes, but it doesn't bring in the contracts that produce big bucks. Look, Dad, I know that you were part of the power structure. You guys were in bed with the politicians, and all of you got rich on sweetheart deals and kickbacks. You scratched each other's balls for fun and profit. So what? I don't fault you. I know how the system works. I just want to be part of it. I want to be on the inside. That's what I really want from you. I want your chair at the big table."

"There is no happiness in it, Theo," Booker advised.

"I'll take my chances," Theo retorted.

"It is not in my power to give you my former

life. I can give you the company and my title, but you must find your own path."

"That's great," Theo responded with resentment. "You are talking about a path when I'm talking about a six-lane interstate highway. Can't you see where I am coming from?"

"I see," Booker said, "and I ask you to slow down, to stop for a while before you rush in any direction. Before you do anything, you need to know who is the doer. I can help you if you will let me. If you want my legacy, take this gift. It is the most valuable thing I possess."

"Take what?" Theo said, getting to his feet. "Take some primitive, spiritual idea that will entitle me to become a supermarket bagboy? Thanks, but no thanks. I can do better on my own. Isn't that what you always said? Be self-reliant? Be smarter and work harder than the other guy?"

"I was wrong," Booker said, looking into Theo's angry face.

"No, Dad. You were right then, but you are wrong now. You are wrong because you are trying to destroy yourself and everything you built. Well, we're not going to let you do that."

Theo charged out of the house, leaving his father seated by the slowly dying fire. The pale light of the rainy afternoon faded into darkness as the outwardly still man struggled to keep his thoughts from ripping open his chest and exposing his human heart. He knew the danger of his own weakness and cried out for holy intervention. When it came, it was like a hot bath to aching knees. The intensity ebbed away, giving him relief from pain. When Buffy arrived home from work, she illuminated the dark family room to discover her father asleep in the fireside chair.

CHAPTER TWENTY-FOUR

The October dawns were often cold with a bitterness born of humidity from the sea that made thirty degrees bone-chilling. Booker purchased a wool-lined rain-resistant parka with a hood for the long walk between Buffy's house and his work at the Winn-Dixie. Every personal item that he required was abundantly available at the shops on Virginia Beach Blvd.

He frequented a Waffle House Restaurant for breakfast at times when he was the sole customer. He chose another small restaurant for meals at the end of his work day, which usually ended at one o'clock. Booker had been promoted to stock clerk for the hours following his early morning unloading duties. Wilson James was still paying him $30 a day off the clock, plus a wage of $6 per hour as a stock clerk. It was an odd-shift forty-eight-hour work week that netted Booker over $300.

The people who saw Booker most working days admired his quiet, gentle nature and were attracted to him as a confidant, although they knew very little about him personally. Those who came to seek his advice did not always understand his counsel, but whatever concern they brought to him was less of a problem when they went away. For reasons they could not put into words, they wanted to return his generosity of spirit with tokens of their own affection.

A truck driver who was a regular at the loading dock pressed on Booker a new pair of work gloves. Booker had grieved with the man over the death of his sister. A waitress at the Waffle House gave Booker a warm wool scarf and treated him as her best customer. He had encouraged her out of a depression brought on by her struggles as a single parent.

Wilson James refused to take Booker's money for the weekly purchase of grits for the Catholic Worker. "I talked to my manager, and the manager at the other store. We've got you covered on this."

At every turn, through every day, Booker was blessed as he recognized the nobility of those with whom he came in contact. In acknowledging each person with his full attention, in full awareness of their connection to him, he energized them to goodness. What was his nature encouraged their own sympathetic natures. In their grief or depression or doubt was a plea for love. Booker was responsive, and what he gave came back multiplied. Whatever seemed wrong with his own situation was being healed in this process of giving and receiving among apparent strangers. Booker found this to be his great joy.

Each day was filled with exciting encounters where this exchange might take place. The clerk in the drug store, having a bad day and resenting whomever she must serve, was arrested by the older man who demonstrated concern for her unhappiness and heard out her frustrations. He touched her hand in charity and she smiled in a transforming release. Her attitude was altered, and she showed gratitude through glistened eyes. The experience was an ecstasy to Booker.

Bill and Buffy did not know the details of their house guest's life. Every day except Sunday, he left the house before they awoke. In the evenings, the working couple most often met for supper at a restaurant before going home. Although Booker was invited, he generally made his own light supper and went to bed by ten because of his 4:00 A.M. rising. On most days, Booker saw his daughter and her husband less than two hours a day. For them, he was the perfect guest. He did his own laundry, fixed his own meals, and cleaned his own room and bathroom.

Ellen and Theo shared the house in Lakewood, but they had little contact with each other. Theo occupied his own room and private bath and, like his mother, took most of his meals out of the house. There was a maid three days a week and a lawn care service for the yard, so neither person had household responsibilities.

Technically, Ellen was Theo's boss, but she required no reports from him. Despite the upheaval of Winn's disappearance, the company was still going to have a highly profitable year. Plantation Estates, a new residential development represented exclusively by Conover Real Estate, sold out its first phase and promised to be strong for years through Phase V. Ellen received a great deal of professional praise for her decorating and staffing of the model homes. She spent her workdays between her Norfolk and Virginia Beach offices and the Plantation Estate sales office. She usually had supper with clients or associates and seldom got home before ten. She felt more secure about her abilities than she ever had before. Her work and her personal life, always a symbiosis, now seemed totally integrated to her. There were busy days when she did not think about her estranged husband.

Theo, despite some panic at the office over his lack of lucrative commercial listings, was enjoying a successful social life. He had found a set of young executive bachelors who justified their progressive entertainments as business networking, although the targets of their attention appeared to be attractive, eligible women they met at bar happy hours. When drinks led to dinner and then to late-hour romance, Theo often did not go home to Lakewood. He slept over at one of his cronies' apartments or with a convenient girlfriend. Theo was sure that these were the best days of his life.

The attorney retained by Ellen to represent her in divorce proceedings was in a quandary concerning a property settlement. He had advised Ellen that a settlement in which her husband received nothing, or even a token share of their estate, might come back to haunt her. At some future date—after a remarriage, for example—he might return to make a claim. A court might hold that he had diminished capacity at the time of the settlement and had been wrongfully deprived of his rightful entitlements. This possibility of Winn coming to his senses about material wealth would hang over Ellen's head if she did not establish a reasonable equity in the settlement.

"Even if he insists on taking nothing, you can't accept it," Ellen was advised.

The accounting process of evaluating the assets of their marriage took more than two weeks. Then there were two long separate sessions with the attorney and CPA to work out the settlement options.

"He will accept whatever we put in front of him," Ellen told them. "He doesn't have an attorney, and he won't hire one."

"That's exactly why we have to be careful," her attorney warned.

In the final draft, Ellen got the Lakewood house, the Nags Head cottage, the car washes, half the stocks and bonds, and the real estate business, assets worth over $2 million, for $678,000 to be paid out over a ten-year period. Most of the $67,800 annual payment to Winn was designed to come directly out of the real estate business.

"You will hardly feel it," her clever CPA assured her.

In addition, Booker as Winn retained the nearly $96,000 invested in his IRA retirement accounts.

"If he signs off on this settlement, you are home free," the attorney said. "If I were working for him, you would have had to sell everything to put a million dollars on the table. The ten-year buy-out would never fly with me."

Booker had to request the day off from Winn-Dixie to keep the 10:00 A.M. appointment at a downtown Norfolk attorney's office. When Theo offered to provide transportation, Booker asked for a 6:30 A.M. pick-up.

"Why so early?" Theo asked with displeasure.

"I want to show you something, and we can have breakfast together," Booker explained.

The ride to Norfolk via the expressway that connected downtown Norfolk with the Virginia Beach oceanfront was made mostly in silence. There was little traffic, but it would build over the next two hours to fill all six westbound lanes. Theo was not used to the early start and functioned like a somnambulist. Like his mother, he usually officially started his day around ten with a second cup of coffee at his desk.

When the journey neared the downtown exits, Booker asked Theo to take Tidewater Drive.

"Where are we going?" Theo asked.

"A few more blocks," Booker encouraged. "Take a left on Princess Anne, and we're almost there."

As the car approached Monticello Avenue, they could see the crowd gathered around one corner of the intersection.

"What's going on here?" Theo said with some alarm.

"It's peaceful," his father reassured him. "Find a place to park. We are going to join them."

"What in the hell are all these people doing down

here at 7:00 in the morning?" Theo asked, still confused.

"They are having breakfast," Booker said simply.

Theo parked the car and got a closer look at the men on the street. "God," he exclaimed. "There are over a hundred of them."

"Thursday is a popular day," Booker recalled. "There are probably two men on the serving line who look a lot like Bartyles and James from the wine cooler commercials."

Theo got out of the car and came around to his father's side, but then hesitated as he noticed details of the men across the street.

"Hey, Dad. We're not dressed for this. Look at those guys. They are street people, bums. It's too cold out here. I think I would rather wait in the car."

"For once in your life, Theo, don't think," Booker advised. "Please come with me. I want you to meet a friend of mine. Don't worry, we'll be welcomed. Everyone is welcomed."

Many eyes followed the pair as they crossed the street. They might have been cops, but the white bearded one in the baggy pants and blue parka seemed harmlessly familiar. The young guy in the suit and overcoat was too well dressed to be a cop, and he seemed nervous. Maybe he was a first-time volunteer. They were always scared of the street.

Booker greeted the men who caught his eye with a warm smile that was sometimes returned. Theo struggled to stay close to his father and deliberately avoided eye contact as they moved through the crowd. A line was forming up ahead, and Theo could smell the hot food. Finally, his father found the man he was looking for.

"Good morning, Bell," Booker said to a small, wiry black man with a face full of curly white beard.

"Do I know you?" Bell asked suspiciously.

"I'm Booker Washington Jones," Booker said with his arms outstretched.

Bell studied the man for a moment in confusion, and then his tense face broke into a broad gap-toothed smile. "Good Lawd, man. You has grown up to be my twin. I didn't know you behind all that hair."

Bell grasped the offered hand and then allowed himself to be pulled into the man's embrace. Booker whispered, "I am very grateful for the help you gave me in May," before he released Bell.

"Bell, this is my son, Theo."

Theo was obviously out of his element, but he extended his hand as manners dictated.

"This boy is better dressed than a Black Bishop on Church Street," Bell said in the way of a compliment. "Where you been all these months?"

"It's a long story," Booker said.

"Nobody round here gives a damn about long stories, so you is spared the excuses," Bell said with a wink.

"How have you been?" Booker asked.

"I'm about half OK. You know. I got my beer loading thing, and there's always food behind the restaurants. I'm hoping for a soft winter. Somebody stole my jacket last week, but I'll get another one from the Salvation Army or something."

Bell's protection against the frigid November morning was a layering of two sweaters, a frayed crew neck covered by a buttoned up cardigan with the holes at the elbows.

Booker began removing his parka. "Please take my jacket," he offered.

Bell seemed stunned by the gesture but allowed Booker to help him into the garment. The right flapped pocket contained $500 in folded $20 bills. Booker had intended the money for Bell if he had found him. The giving of the parka provided an unexpected way of conveying the gift. Standing behind Bell holding the parka as his friend found the ample sleeve openings, Booker leaned in to whisper, "There is something for you in the pocket."

With the parka on, Bell seemed to be testing the pockets when he felt the money. He was too wise to show it in a crowd, but he was excited by its potential. Even if it were only five dollar bills, it was a lot of money, especially from a man who he recalled as more destitute than himself.

Booker saw the thought on Bell's face. "It's OK. I've got a good job and a crib at my daughter's. I can get another coat."

"You cast your bread . . . ," Bell said in wonder.

"Exactly," Booker affirmed.

"What are you guys talking about?" Theo asked in bewilderment.

"It's about giving and receiving being the same thing," Booker said.

"Let's eat. I can smell the soup," Bell said.

The three men fell in at the end of the line and

shuffled toward the curbside serving area. Bell took his full measure of the hot soup, sandwich, and coffee. Booker followed, and when he accepted a sandwich from the man known to the street people as Bartyles, he shook the man's hand. "Please accept our small gratitude to support your service." When the hand came away, Bartyles was surprised to find two fifty dollar bills in his palm. Booker moved on before the man could thank him.

Theo stayed tight on his father through the line but seemed embarrassed by the hand-outs. He would accept only a cup of coffee. Then he stood against the warehouse wall while his father and his street person friend sat on the curb talking and enjoying their meal. The cold wind whipping up Monticello Avenue forced the remaining people on the street to huddle together as they ate. The food givers were already packing up their vehicles. Theo noticed that his coatless father was shivering involuntarily.

Booker felt his son standing over him and then the draping of the camel hair overcoat over his shoulders. He turned to thank Theo, but the boy was already walking toward the car.

"Nice boy," Bell observed. "He's built just like you."

"Yes," Booker acknowledged. "I know."

Booker would have liked to have seen Steve, but the originator of the feeding program had emergency duties that morning with one of the mentally ill indigents he hosted in his home.

Bell saw Booker to Theo's car and waved them goodbye. When they were gone, he found a secluded alley and looked at the money in the parka for the first time. He counted it twice in delighted shock. If he was careful, the windfall would provide for a warm, cozy winter. Bell hurried toward Church Street to share the story of his good fortune with his new best friend, Woody. Woody had the crib, and Bell now had the heat. "Blow wind, blow," he said out loud. "Ole Bell ain't afraid of you no more."

CHAPTER TWENTY-FIVE

Since it was still two hours before their meeting, Theo suggested that he drive his father to Lakewood where he could pick up one of his overcoats.

"You've got some beautiful cashmere coats," Theo reminded him. "And while we're there, you might want to put on a better suit. Pardon me, but the suit you are wearing looks like it came from a rummage sale."

"Do you like the clothes at the house?" Booker asked.

"Of course," Theo responded. "They are the best you can buy."

"Then you can have them. And what you can't use, I would like you to donate to the Catholic Worker."

"But why? And we're not Catholic," Theo responded.

"Why, because I don't need those kinds of garments anymore. And the Catholic Worker, because they once showed me a great kindness, and they will place the clothes where they are most needed."

"Don't you want anything from the house? What about your golf clubs, your jewelry?"

"Really, Son, I can't use them."

Theo was silent for a while. "So where do you want to go?"

"Let's find a coffee shop where you can get some breakfast. I might drink a second cup of coffee myself."

Theo parked the Explorer in a downtown garage near the lawyer's office building and selected a nearby coffee shop to wait till the appointment time. After Theo finished his eggs, he asked, "Do you know what is going to happen this morning?"

"I think so," his father said.

"Mother is divorcing you." Theo spoke in a tone he might use with a retarded person in an attempt to force a fact into his head.

"I know that."

"They are going to offer you a settlement. They have been working on it for weeks. Do you know what is involved?" Theo kept his voice low, but it was intense.

"No, I don't," Booker said. "It is not important. Whatever your mother feels is appropriate is fine with me. There is no conflict."

"You are so complacent," Theo complained. "It's like you are a whipped dog, and you will take anything that they dish out."

"Is that so?" Booker inquired.

"Well," Theo said qualifying his previous remark, "it seems so."

"Son, my whole purpose in returning was to help you and your mother and Buffy come to a peaceful resolution concerning my change of life. I could not know the nature of the resolution. It had to unfold according to your individual needs. Whatever occurs is appropriate. I am just the observer in this process. I cannot be in conflict with you. If this behavior is puzzling, I can understand."

"But you have no defense," Theo said. "You have no position."

"My strength is in my defenselessness," Booker said smiling. "It is an old truth you may someday learn for yourself."

Two third-generation attorneys waited with Ellen around a polished mahogany conference table designed to seat twelve. The room was lined with bookshelves, and there was a grouping of four Queen Anne chairs with lamp tables at the end of the long room. The room was calculated to resemble the exclusive ambiance of an English men's club of the previous century.

Booker as Winn knew the principals of the large firm socially, but he did not recognize the younger partners who specialized in divorce. Formal introductions were made, and the party of five sat down at places indicated by neat stacks of legal documents. The newcomers were offered coffee or tea from a silver service on a convenience sideboard, but declined.

The senior of the two attorneys opened by acknowledging the uncontested divorce based on a separation dating from May 18. There were documents to sign, of course, but Winn would not be required to appear in court. Secondly, there the matter of the property settlement which would be

gone over in detail. If none of the items was con-
tested, the attorney said he was prepared to present
Winn with a cashier's check for the first year's payment.

It took just an hour to read the assembled documents to Winn and to secure his signatures.
Witnesses from nearby offices were brought in to
attest to Winn's participation and signed documents making the settlement self-proofing. The attorneys regarded this maneuver as their trump
card should the husband later decide to contest
the settlement.

Ellen remained composed, although she did not
look directly at her husband during the proceeding.
Theo was silent throughout. When the deed was
done, Booker went to his ex-wife and embraced her.
Only then did she begin to weep. When he and
Theo departed, the senior attorney said, "Congratu-
lations, Ms. Conover, you are a free woman. I wish
all divorce settlements were this easy. Believe me,
your former husband was a pussycat. And I mean
that with all due respect."

In the car on the expressway back to Virginia
Beach, the finality of what he had witnessed hit
Theo, and his emotions welled up in his eyes.

"I can't believe this is happening," he moaned.

"All things happen for a purpose," his father said.
"Hold on to what is changeless. Be kind to your
mother and your sister, and know that my love for
all of you never changes."

"But what will you do?" Theo asked.

"First, I have to give Wilson James at least a

week's notice at the supermarket. Then I will go back to Santa Fe."

"Why do you have to go back there?" Theo asked as a lament.

"You are not being abandoned," Booker reassured his son. "A person should be able to find happiness and fulfillment anywhere and under any circumstances if he understands the purpose of the experience. But I am weak. The mind still competes with the heart and my peace is not complete. In Santa Fe, I have a wise brother to comfort me and a simple lifestyle that put the active, aggressive man to sleep. If your hardship and that of your mother and sister are to mean anything, I must fulfill my mission."

"I'm not sure I understand what you mean by your mission," Theo said. "Why is it so important?"

Booker smiled, recognizing his own doubts and questions. "The mission is every person's mission. What we all deeply desire for ourselves is liberation from fear and conflict so that we can experience unqualified happiness. I have found the door to this bliss. If a person like me, raised and practiced in materialism and the pursuit of power and pleasure, can open the door to divine compassion, there is hope for us all. I believe that this is our ultimate destiny. The road we have made so long and so torturous is based on a colossal error. We thought that we were separate from our Creator, and therefore separate from each other. It's a terrible lie that we invented and then came to cherish. Son, the Truth is what sets us free."

Theo could not assimilate the concepts his father was articulating. The semantics were too complex and became muddled in the vocabulary of Theo's Christian Sunday School education. Was his father seriously trying to be Jesus? And if he was, wasn't that a sacrilege? Cult leaders claimed to be Jesus. They were dangerous and pitifully insane. Where was his father on this totem? It was too disturbing for Theo to dwell on, so he changed the subject.

"I have to get back to the office," Theo said.

"Of course," Booker agreed, realizing that his spontaneous preaching had been unsuccessful in converting Theo. Sermons and rituals had not enlightened the world since time began. Booker saw them powerless even given the best intentions. For the rest of the trip, he sought the place of peace within himself and trusted its power to communicate that which he could not.

CHAPTER TWENTY-SIX

The morning after the settlement, Booker told Wilson James that he would be able to work only one more week.

"I knew it was too good to last," Wilson said in disappointment. "I guess I'm being selfish in wanting you to stay. You've made my job easier. You made me look forward to coming to work. What supermarket night manager can say that?"

"Your happiness is not dependent on me," Booker said. "Whatever you see in me is a reflection of your own Self. If I have served you well, it is only because you opened the door to me. You first gave me your trust and confidence. All I did was return these gifts to you."

"You talk like The Book," Wilson said. "I see the principles, but they are so damn hard to practice. You see what I have to deal with—undereducated adults, kids who resent work, employees who will try to steal more than they earn. How can I be a sheep among wolves?"

"First ask, who are the sheep, and who are the wolves?" Booker continued, as the first truck of the morning backed into the dock.

"And who sees the conflict?" Booker concluded.

The conversation ended as the men went to work. Wilson James had a feeling that he was just about to understand something profound, but the moment passed as he moved on to the details of his job. He appreciated Booker Jones as a very unusual man, a humble, wise man who had changed the workplace with his ethic and his consideration for others. Everyone at the store who had worked with Booker would regret his leaving. Wilson wondered if he could maintain the harmony of his shift employees once Booker had gone. He concluded that it was up to him. It had always been up to him. Maybe this time, he thought, he was up to the responsibility.

Booker as Winn waited until Monday afternoon to open a money market account at a national brokerage firm where he deposited the settlement check. The interest-earning account allowed its owner to write up to five checks a month. It was a convenient way to handle the money, especially if it was not needed for upkeep expenses.

The travel agent's office was in the same shopping center as the branch office of the stock brokerage firm. Booker paid cash for a one-way airline ticket leaving Norfolk early Sunday morning following his last day of work at Winn-Dixie. The travel agent offered to make accommodation and rental car reservations, but Booker told her that they were not needed.

Buffy had been weepy on the evening of her parents' divorce and had been torn between which one of them to console. Ellen, who had made dinner plans for the conscious purpose of not being alone, released her daughter to tend to her former husband. Buffy and Bill, therefore, came directly home from work with two large white bags of hot food secured from a Chinese take-out. Booker as Winn greeted them with his usual warmth, seemingly unconscious of the drama that the two young people expected to unfold.

The Port of Hampton Roads, which rolled out the men and materials of war on a century of tides, also attracted to itself the ethnic peoples who experienced its outflow. Consequently, there were very good oriental restaurants in Norfolk and Virginia Beach. If a certain restaurateur whispered to the host of a dinner party that he had prepared Peking Duck in the same manner for Chairman Mao, he could be believed. If the owner claimed to have been an aeronautical engineer or a medical doctor in his or her own country, that was also probable.

Buffy had sought to please her father with dishes from his favorite Chinese restaurant. The food she brought home was exquisite. When the squat cartons were opened on the kitchen counters, they seemed to occupy every space. She had ordered three entrees, soups, egg rolls, and both white and fried rice. It was too much to eat even for excessive Western appetites.

The three people fixed their own plates buffet-style and then assembled at the seldom used dining room table. Buffy and Bill talked about their work day in a strained attempt to effect normalcy. Finally, urged on by eye contact from his wife, Bill addressed the subject that compromised their lifestyle.

"What do you think you will do now?" Bill ventured. "Do you want to stay with us a while longer or start looking for a place of your own?"

"You have been very generous," Booker began. "Perhaps you would let me stay another eight or ten days, and then I will be gone."

"Of course, Daddy," Buffy said quickly. "You are always welcome here."

"And you are always welcomed wherever I am," Booker replied.

"And where will that be?" Bill asked cautiously.

"I believe that I will go back to Santa Fe if you have no need of me here," Booker replied.

"We could visit you there," Buffy said with some enthusiasm. "We've been to California, but I always wanted to see Santa Fe. We'd have to stay in a hotel, though. I'm not ready to use an outhouse."

"I understand," her father said.

"But we would like to meet the Indians," Bill offered.

"Of course," Booker said. "They are not very talkative, but there is much to learn from them."

"Great," Buffy said with relief. "We'll come out there for a few days the next vacation we take."

"Fine," Booker agreed. "Your mother would be welcomed, too."

Buffy exchanged glances with Bill before she spoke. "I don't think we can expect her to visit Santa Fe for a long time."

"Then perhaps Theo will come," Booker speculated.

"Don't expect Theo either, Dad," Buffy said with

some hesitation. "He's in a very angry place right now, although he's the only winner in this disaster. He's got your job, your car. He's never had it so good. But he's not grateful. If you listen to Theo, you'd think that he was carrying the weight of the world on his shoulders."

"It doesn't seem to hinder his night life," Bill observed.

"He's confused," Buffy countered. "He's under a lot of pressure."

"He will find his way," Booker said.

"Sure he will," Buffy agreed. "It will just take a while."

The Winn-Dixie people had a cake for Booker at nine o'clock Saturday morning. There were only five fellow employees including Wilson James to say goodbye, but no one could remember a similar gesture being accorded a part-time stock clerk and bag boy ever before. As a going away present, Wilson promised that the Catholic Worker grits program would continue as long as there was a street feeding.

"Me and the Norfolk store manager are going down there on my next day off to see what is going on for ourselves," Wilson promised.

The manager offered to take Booker home after the brief party, but he declined. The final handshake in the parking lot turned into a hug with Wilson James at a loss to express his sentiment. He watched the older man walk toward the shopping center in his blue replacement parka. The day would be surprisingly mild for November 11, but the early morning had been cold. Wilson James watched his former employee until he was out of sight. He felt a longing in his chest and an urge to follow Booker Jones to wherever he was going. Then he judged the emotion as excessively sentimental, got into his car, and went home.

Booker's personal belongings still fit into the backpack he had purchased near the Greensboro truck stop after his first job as a lumper. He packed just after dawn on Sunday morning and then took a walk in Buffy's neighborhood. He had his Indian style breakfast of grits, stewed fruit, and herbal tea ready for Buffy and Bill when they came downstairs. Sunday was normally the couples' sleep-in day, so the hour was rude enough without the thought of the ride to the Norfolk airport and the potentially emotional departure. Booker's flight was scheduled to depart at 8:24 A.M.

Theo had told Buffy that he would meet them at the airport to see their father off. The airport was only fifteen minutes from Lakewood. The most awkward moments of the morning occurred as Buffy held her father at the departure gate until the last moments for boarding, anticipating in vain the late arrival of her brother. He did not come.

There was a last-minute embrace, unsatisfying to Buffy, and her father, gentle and uncritical to the last, was gone. Buffy wept as much over the loss of a satisfying farewell as she did in anger toward Theo.

"That self-centered bastard," she cried in Bill's arms. "He promised me he would be here. I can't believe he would hurt Daddy like this."

"I think your daddy is beyond that kind of injury," Bill said. "He's not at the effect of the stupid behaviors that torment us. He's above it, Honey."

"I hope so," Buffy replied, looking into her husband's face, "but that doesn't mean that Theo is forgiven by me."

"Forget about it," Bill said as he took his wife's arm and led her toward the terminal exit. "Let's go get some real breakfast. Your daddy may have gone native, but when I eat grits, I want to see some eggs and bacon on the side."

Buffy laughed through her tears. "And some coffee. I almost gagged on that awful tea."

Booker's flight to Albuquerque changed in Dallas with about an hour's layover. During the wait, his mind was quiet, not choosing to recall or analyze what had happened in Norfolk. Nevertheless, he was very alert. The mind, freed from its unproductive preoccupations, was a bright window with a wondrous view of the human landscape. Amid the throngs of people rushing or impatiently waiting in the airport terminal, Booker saw a young mother overburdened with a baby in arms, a resisting toddler at hand, and a purse and diaper bag too large to manage. Scores of people, including women who had once had children themselves, passed the troubled woman as she sat overwrought by her task.

"May I help you?" Booker asked.

The young mother paused, seemingly weighing her suspicions against her need. The older man in the white beard, jeans, cowboy boots, and hat could be a Texas rancher, a grandfather.

"Yes. Thank you. I'm about to miss my flight. I just came in from Birmingham, and I don't know where to go. Little Ray has been a terror. He's in his terrible twos. He had a tantrum a few minutes ago. I'm exhausted."

"I understand," Booker said. "May I see your ticket?"

The woman handed over her ticket as Little Ray stopped squirming to stare up at the strange cowboy with the short Santa Claus beard.

"My name is Sue. This is baby Rachel and Little Ray. Their daddy just made sergeant in the army. We're on our way to join him," she said.

"San Antonio," Booker said, reading the ticket and checking the flight information monitor mounted in the corridor ceiling.

"He's an army medic. We're going to be at Fort Sam Houston," she explained. "This is our first trip on an airplane."

"It can be confusing," Booker acknowledged. "Let's get started toward your gate. We can make your flight. Don't worry."

Booker asked Little Ray if he could carry him and then picked up the boy and the diaper bag and led Sue to another concourse where her flight was already boarding.

"I never would have made it without you," Sue said in parting. "You're an angel."

Booker waved them out of sight and then hoisted his backpack and returned to his own concourse where he just made his own flight. Settled in her seat, Sue realized that she did not know the name of her benefactor.

Within an hour of his arrival in Albuquerque, he was on a bus to Santa Fe. It was still early afternoon in the Mountain Time Zone. The great expanse of blue sky over the western desert was a welcomed sight. Booker saw the mesquite and the piñon trees along his route. The air seemed to be fragrant from a thousand hearth fires.

In Santa Fe, Booker changed to the familiar local line bus that he used to come and go from the pueblo. The bus driver recognized him. "Have you been sick, amigo? I haven't seen you for months."

"I am well, thank you," Booker said. "I had to make a trip."

The bus stopped at the entrance road to the pueblo, and Booker put on the backpack and carried his parka for the walk down the dusty dirt road. The adobe structures rose on the horizon against the backdrop of the mountains where Chief Old Woman was enshrined. The village was quiet. There were only six cars in the visitor parking lot. Somewhere, sitting against a wall facing the afternoon sun, Joseph was offering his private counsel to members of the tribe. Booker had an idea where to find him.

CHAPTER TWENTY-SEVEN

Booker came around the corner of the adobe building and saw Joseph from a distance. A young Indian couple was just departing. No additional tribe members waited for their cacique. Booker set his backpack, parka, and hat on the ground and approached Joseph. As he grew closer and stepped on a twig, the priest did not open his eyes or alter his seated position against the wall. His face remained relaxed, the deep wrinkles catching the afternoon sun like a bronze sculpture.

Booker eased into a seated position beside Joseph and joined him in the silence and sunlight. After more than twenty minutes, the old Indian spoke. "There will be joy among our people that Anglo Who Became Chief Old Woman's Son has found his way home. And yet there are ripples of the past life."

"Your heart sees like an eagle," Booker admitted. "My son rejects our path."

"It is often the way," Joseph said. "Young men must fall before they can stand tall within themselves."

"I may never see him again," Booker said.

"That may happen," the old Indian replied, "but he will probably come someday. He will come in search of the father. If you are not in the body, our clan will tell him the legend of Anglo Who Became Chief Old Woman's Son, and he will find peace and understanding. All will come to understand. The Great Spirit waits in loving patience. Can we do less?"

There was another long period of silence finally broken by Booker. "I have too much money. Can we find a use for it?"

"There are always needs," Joseph began. "Many people will not ask for help, so we must watch carefully to see where we can be of service. In our clan, it is considered shameful if we fail to see our brother's need and do not attempt to help him."

"Are there present needs?" Booker asked.

"Pink Flower Blooming's milk cow has died. Little Strong Hands cannot pay for his truck repairs. Lone Pine Standing needs a new roof on her house. These are worthy needs."

"They will be met," Booker pledged.

"Pearl Found In The River will want to make piki bread now that you have returned. We will have a feast," Joseph said with a great smile.

"And I will climb the mountain and visit my Mother," Booker added.

The two men became silent again, realizing that speech was not able to convey the depth of their feeling. The sun had dipped behind a mountain rim, and the horizon was painted in shades of violet before Joseph spoke again.

"Carlos Silva has asked to come into the priest council. It is a long apprenticeship and a whole-life commitment. He has waited for you to be his guide."

Booker was surprised, but contained his emotion.

"How can I be his guide?"

"Do not concern yourself with the rituals. These things we can teach. Be with him in his meditations. Strengthen him in the sweat lodge. Answer the questions of his heart. This is the real work of the guide. Did Nita lecture to you? And yet she gave you her wisdom. Do as much for Carlos, and he will call you Father."

"They are all our sons," Booker said. "And all our daughters."

"When could we ever be lonely?" Joseph asked.

ABOUT THE AUTHOR

Monty Joynes is a career consumer magazine editor and publisher beginning with *Metro Magazine* and concluding with *Holiday*, the national travel magazine. He has co-authored five titles in the *Insiders' Guide* series and two produced film scripts. *Naked Into the Night* is his first published novel, and its sequel, *Lost in Las Vegas*, is written. Monty lives with his wife, Pat, in Boone, North Carolina.

Hampton Roads Publishing Company
publishes books on a variety of subjects,
including metaphysics, health, integrative medicine,
visionary fiction, and other related topics.
For a copy of our latest catalog, call toll-free,
(800) 766-8009, or send your name and address to:

Hampton Roads Publishing Company, Inc.
134 Burgess Lane
Charlottesville, VA 22902